for 1000+ tutorials ... use our
free site .... drawinghowtodraw.com

Copyright © Rachel A. Goldstein, DrawingHowToDraw.com, 2016

All rights reserved. No part of this book may be reproduced or transmitted in any form or by any means whatsoever without express written permission from the author, except in the case of brief quotations embodied in critical articles and reviews. Please refer all pertinent questions to the publisher. All rights reserved. No part of this book may be reproduced or transmitted in any form or by any means, electronic or mechanical, including photocopying, recording, or by an information storage and retrieval system - except by a reviewer who may quote brief passages in a review to be printed in a magazine or newspaper - without permission in writing from the publisher.

BY RACHEL GOLDSTEIN

ART DRAWING GAMES AND ACTIVITIES FOR KIDS

HUGE ACTIVITY BOOK TO PROMPT CREATIVITY AND SILLY DRAWINGS

GRAPES PROMPT

Use the boring grapes picture (on the next page) to start your imagination churning. Below is an example drawing...but imagine up your own picture!

3D WIZARD BEARD

Finish this drawing of a wizard with his trusty owl. Then turn the page over and give him a 3-d beard!!!

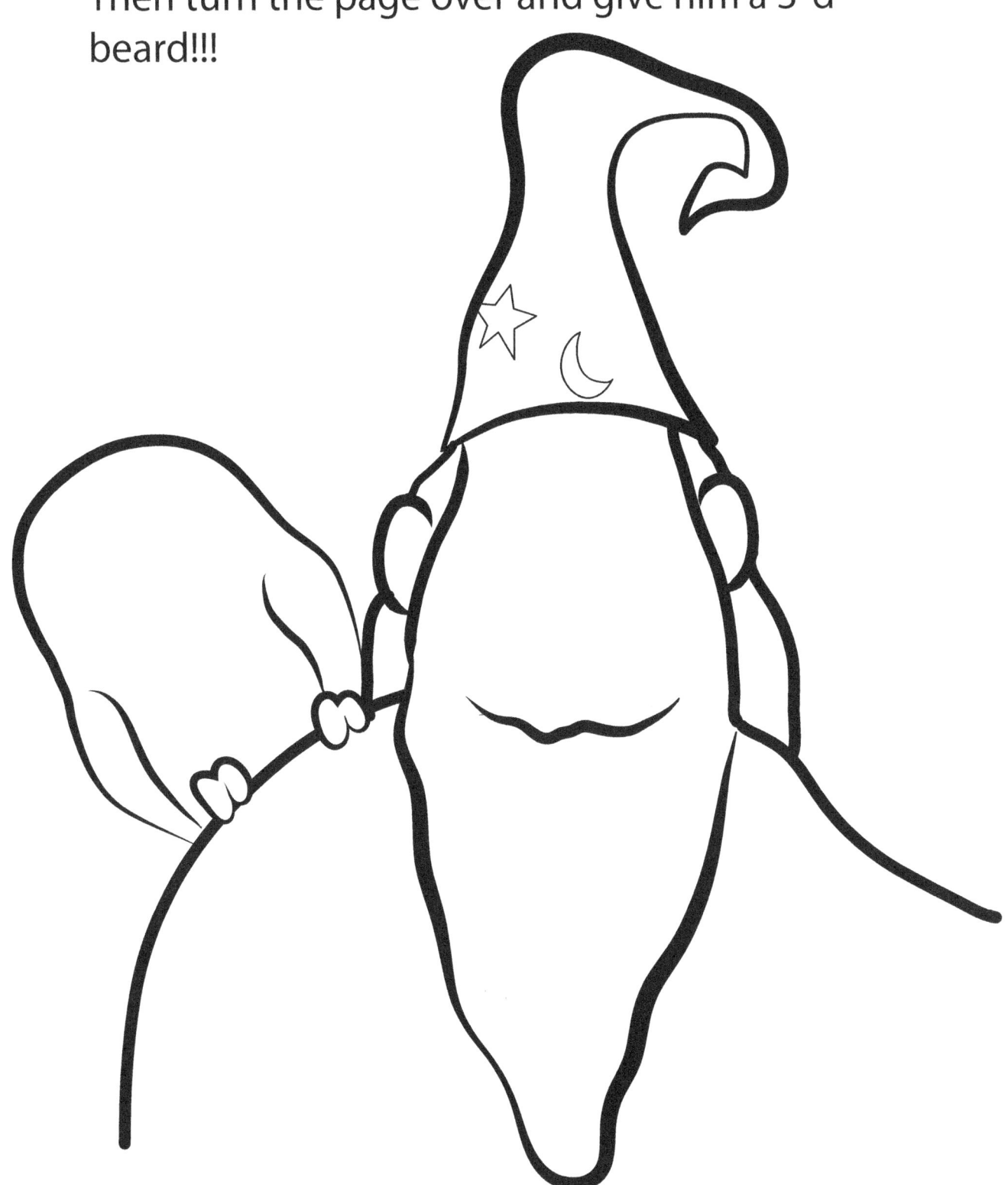

Use your pencil to poke holes behind the beard and the owl to make it look like feathers and whiskers.

DRAW A FACE

Draw a cartoon face from the word "face"!

6.

↓ NOW YOU TRY ↓

DRAWING HANGMAN

This is a 2 player game. Play it just like normal hangman, except you won't be drawing a body part every time a letter is chosen incorrectly. Instead, when a letter is chosen incorrectly, the player needs to draw a step of the tutorial that is on that page. The player loses if the entire tutorial is completed.

1. Player 1 thinks of a word. This player counts how many letters are in the word. This player then scribbles out any extra spaces. So, for example, if the word is "Bologna" (7 letters), then Player 1 would scribble out 5 of the spaces so that only 7 spaces were remaining.

__ __ __ __ __ __ __ ~~~~~~~~~~~~

2. If Player 2 guesses a letter that is incorrect, then he or she has to draw a step in the tutorial that is included. So, if this was the tutorial set included...

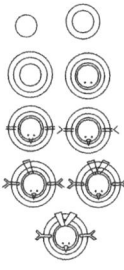

Then Player 2 would draw this the first time they got a letter wrong.

3. Player 2 wins if he or she guess the word correctly. Player 1 wins if Player 2 doesn't guess the word before getting completely through the tutorial.

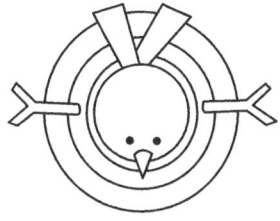

DRAWING HANGMAN

Scribble out any extra spaces.

_ _ _ _ _ _ _ _ _ _ _ _

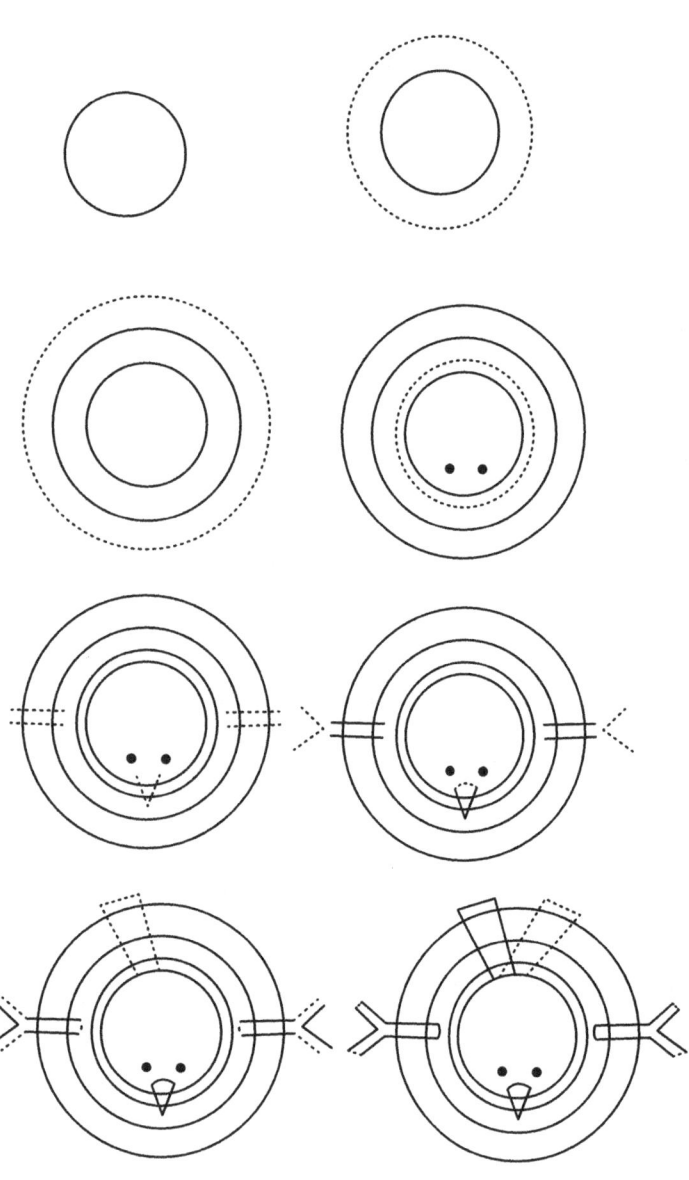

LETTERS

A B C D E F G H I J
K L M N O P Q R S
T U V W X Y Z

DRAW HERE

DRAWING HANGMAN

_ _ _ _ _ _ _ _ _
Scribble out any extra spaces.

LETTERS

ABCDEFGHIJ
KLMNOPQRS
TUVWXYZ

DRAW HERE

DRAWING HANGMAN

_ _ _ _ _ _ _ _ _ _
Scribble out any extra spaces.

LETTERS

A B C D E F G H I J
K L M N O P Q R S
T U V W X Y Z

DRAW HERE

DRAWING HANGMAN

_ _ _ _ _ _ _ _ _ _ _ _ _
Scribble out any extra spaces.

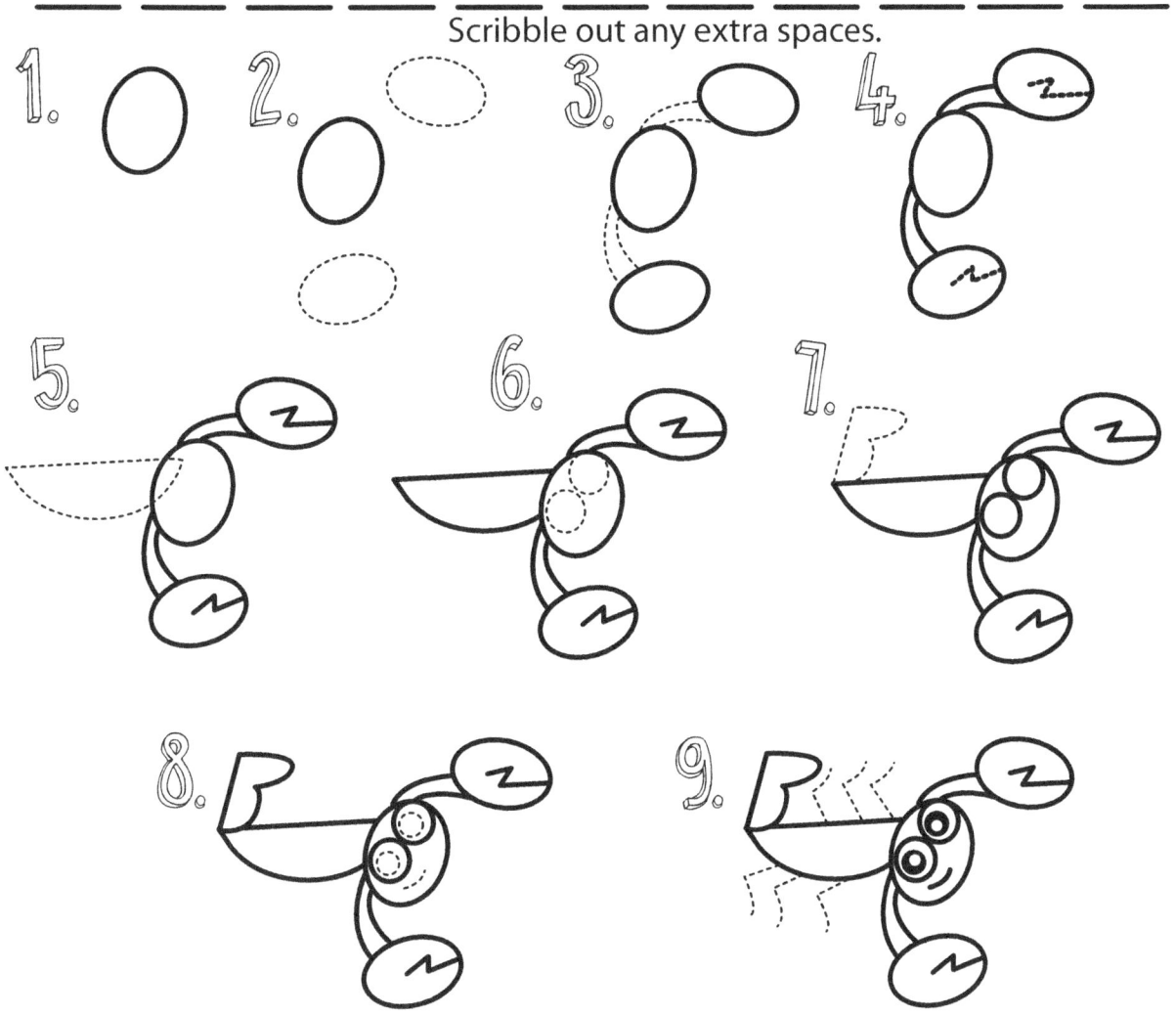

LETTERS

A B C D E F G H I J
K L M N O P Q R S
T U V W X Y Z

DRAW HERE

SCRIBBLE GAME

The Scribble Game is a favorite in my family. We always play this game on vacation, at restaurants, and when we are bored. One player scribbles on a sheet of paper and then hands the paper to the other player. That player then has to form a drawing from this scribble. There are no winners, but there are a lot of giggles. The next few pages have scribbles on them for you to play alone with.

SCRIBBLE GAME

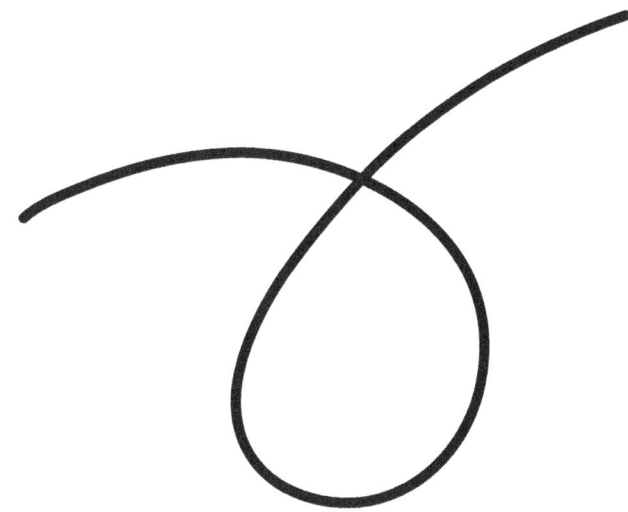

SCRIBBLE GAME

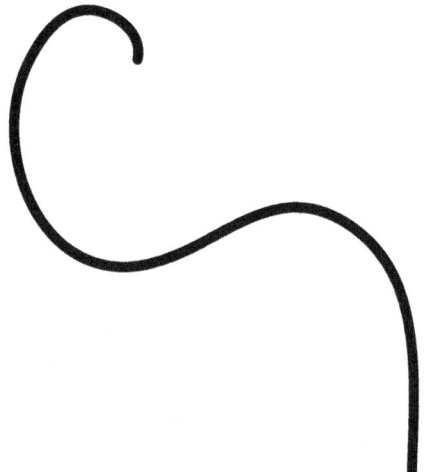

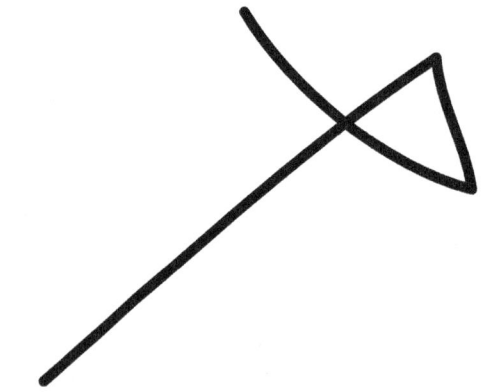

SCRIBBLE GAME

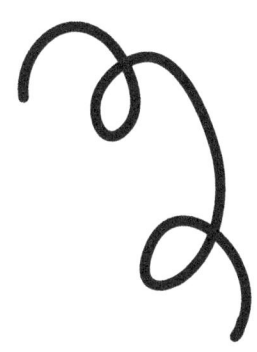

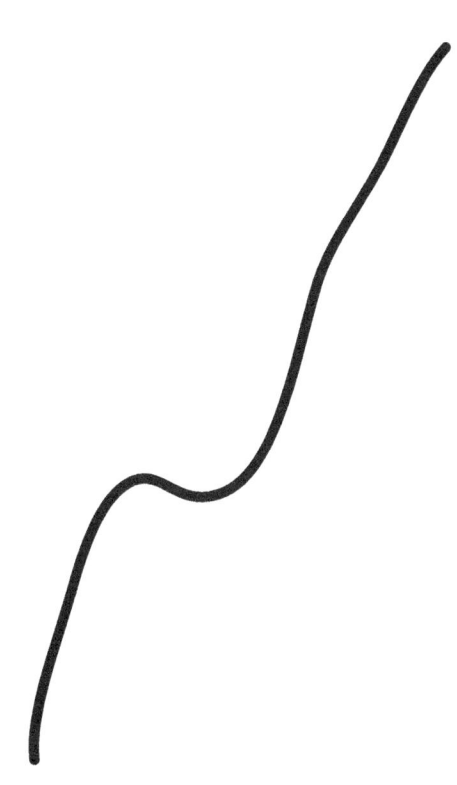

FIVE DOTS

Lets play the five dots game. On the following page you will see a bunch of groupings of dots. Each grouping includes 5 dots. Your task is to draw a person or figure from each grouping of dots. There is a dot for the head, for each hand, and for each foot. See what sorts of figures you can come up with!

FIVE DOTS

FIVE DOTS

FIVE DOTS

DRAWING COOTIE CATCHER

On the following pages you will find a few cootie catcher games. If you have never seen one, I'm sure your parents can clue you in how to play. These are super fun to play with!

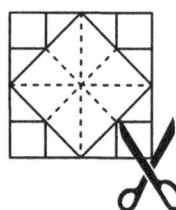 Cut out the square.   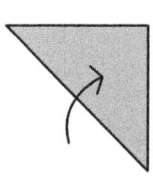 Fold over.

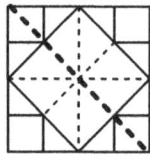 Unfold.   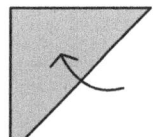 Fold over.   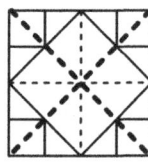 Unfold.

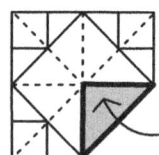 Fold all 4 Corners to Center.    So it Looks Like This.    Keep Folds Together & Turn Over.

 Now Fold All the Corners in Again.   Until it Looks Like This.   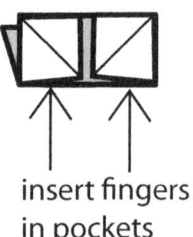 Fold in half inwards.
insert fingers in pockets

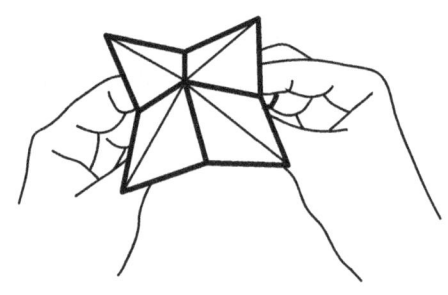 Now you should rotate your hands, bringing your thumbs and index fingers together. Now the cootie catcher should expand and then shrink back again.

DRAWING COOTIE CATCHER

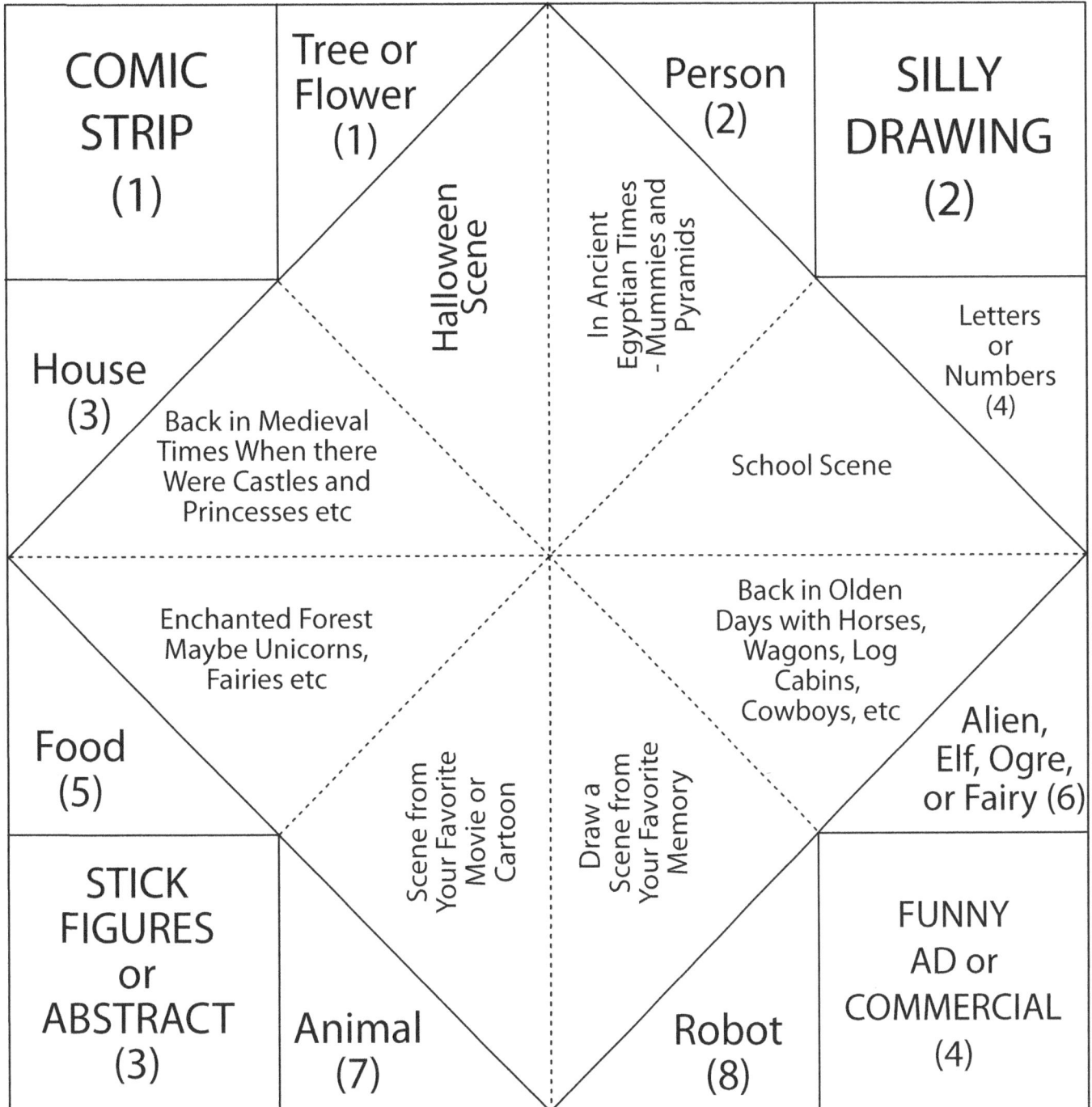

(1) Ask a partner to pick a number. Whatever number they choose is the type of drawing that they have to draw. Pinch and Pull the Cootie Catcher opened and closed the number of times that they chose. Tell the partner the numbers available for them to choose.
(2) Ask partner to choose another number. Tell them the word that is next to that chosen number. The partner should draw that item too. Pinch and Pull the Cootie Catcher opened and closed the number of times that they chose.
(3) Then open up the cootie catcher and give the partner the 2 options that are inside the cootie catcher. Your partner then gets to choose which one of these he wants to draw.

FACES COOTIE CATCHER

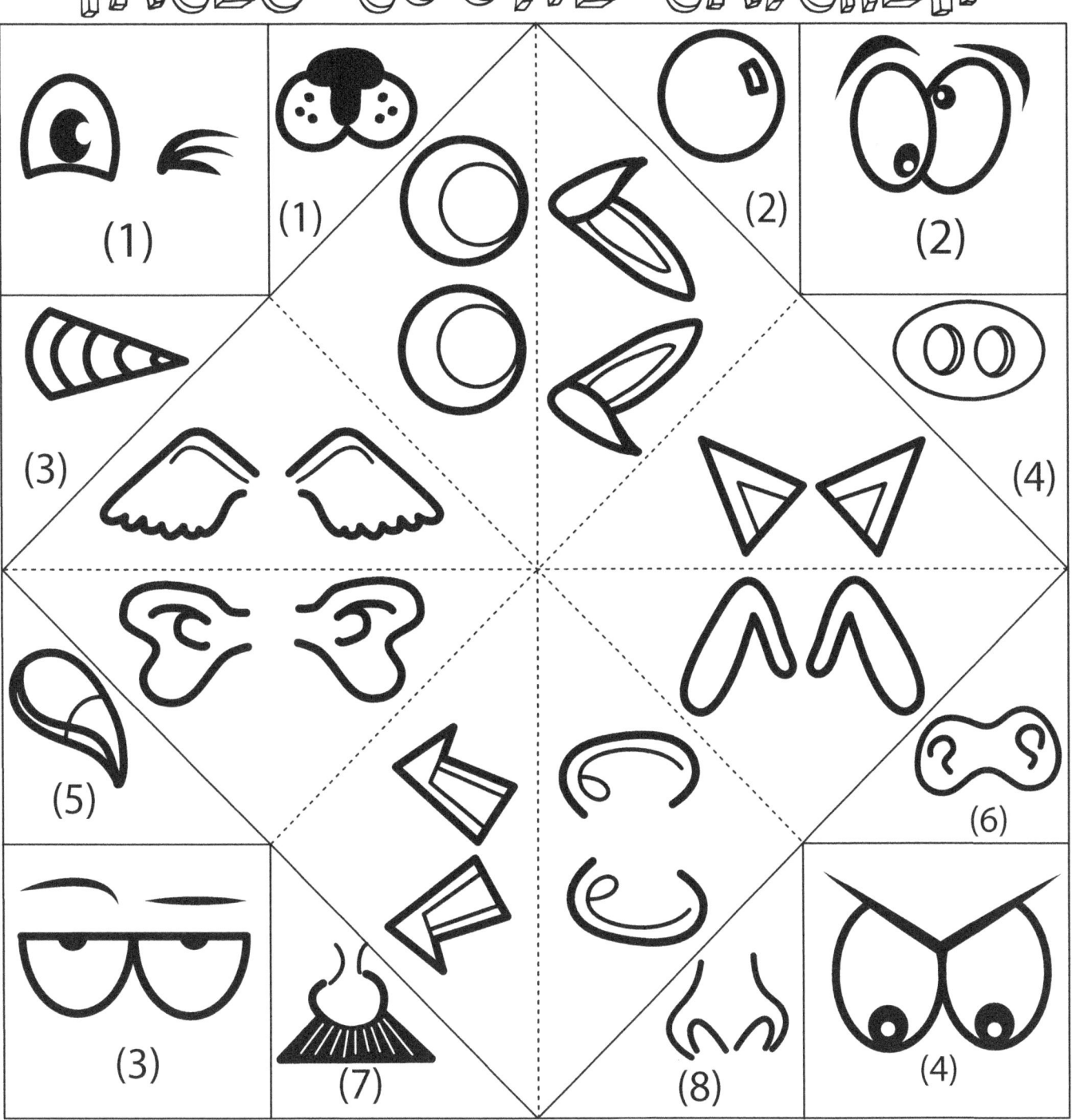

(1) Ask a partner to pick a number. Whatever number they choose is the type of eyes that they have to draw. Show them the eyes and let them draw them. Pinch and Pull the Cootie Catcher opened and closed the number of times that they chose. Tell the partner the numbers available for them to choose.

(2) Ask partner to choose another number. Show them the nose that is next to that chosen number. The partner should draw that nose too. Pinch and Pull the Cootie Catcher opened and closed the number of times that they chose.

(3) Then open up the cootie catcher and show your partner the 2 options that are inside the cootie catcher. Your partner then gets to choose which one of these 2 ears he wants to draw.

MONSTER COOTIE CATCHER

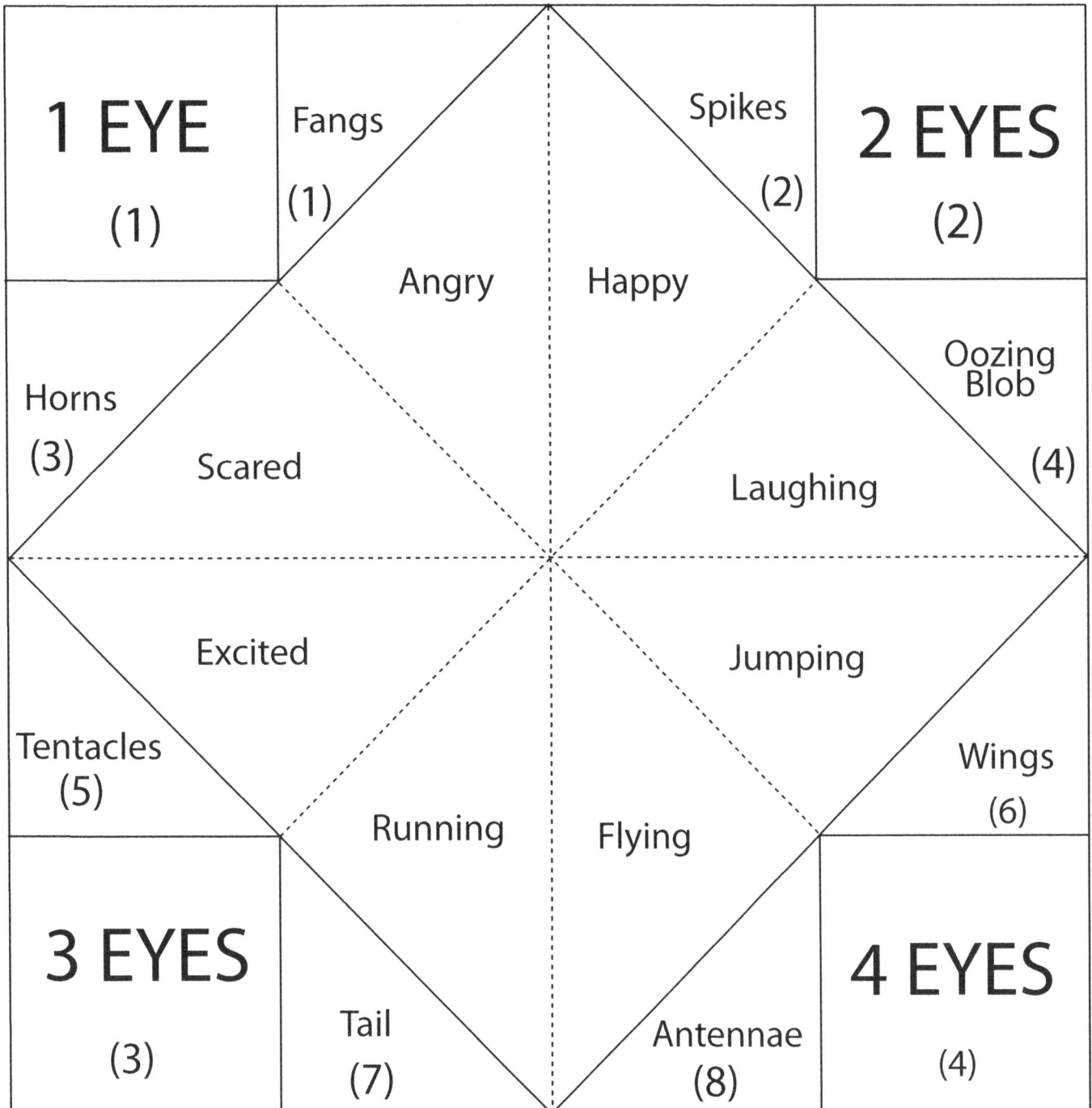

(1) Ask a partner to pick a number. Whatever number they choose is how many eyes their monster has. The partner should draw the eyes. Pinch and Pull the Cootie Catcher opened and closed the number of times that they chose. Tell the partner the numbers available for them to choose.
(2) Ask partner to choose another number. Tell them the word that is next to that chosen number. The partner should draw that item too. Pinch and Pull the Cootie Catcher opened and closed the number of times that they chose.
(3) Then open up the cootie catcher and give the partner the 2 options that are inside the cootie catcher (for example, Running / Flying). Your partner then gets to choose which one of these he wants to draw.

YOUR COOTIE CATCHER

Invent Your Own Cootie Catcher!

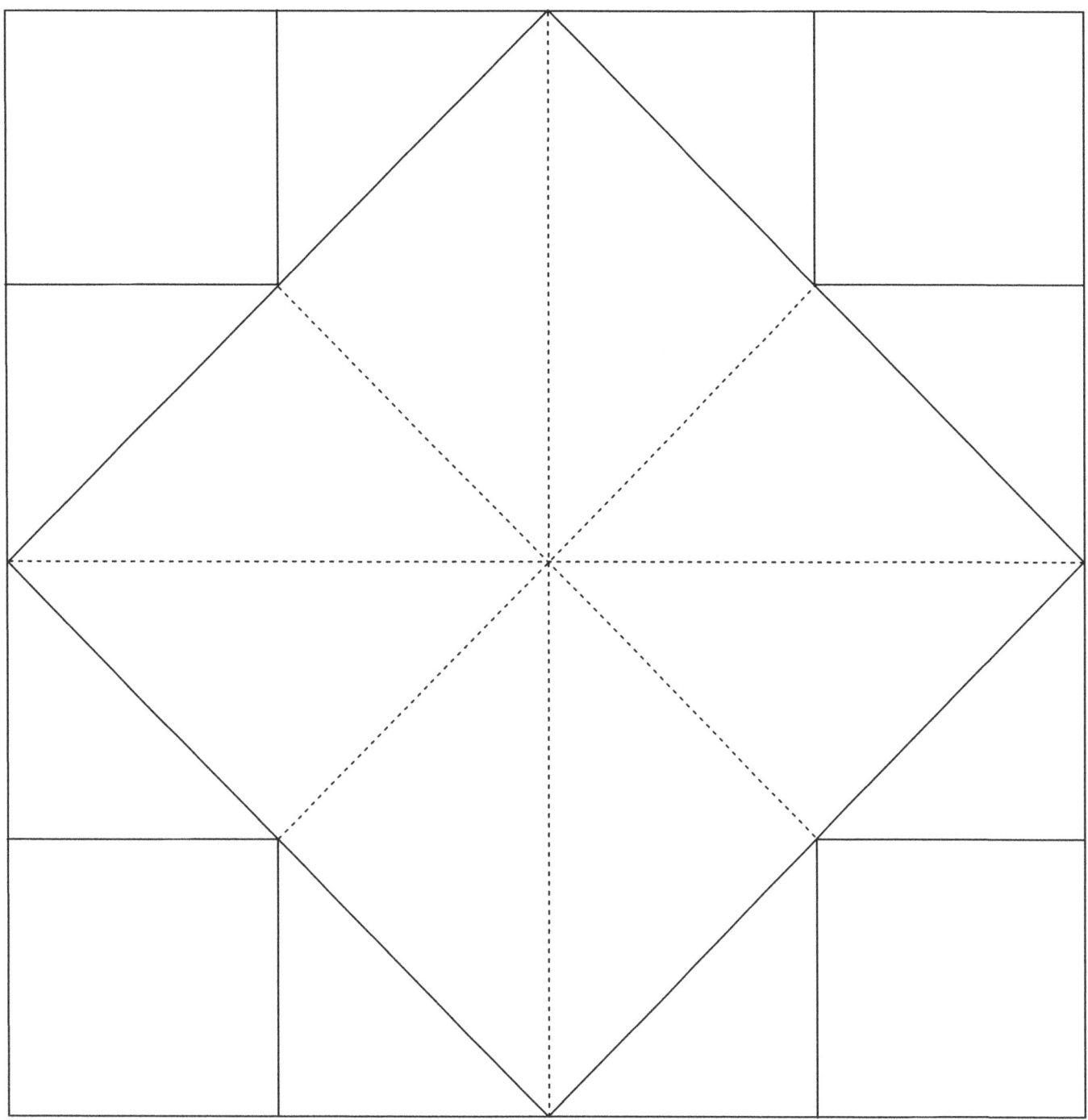

YOUR COOTIE CATCHER

Invent Your Own Cootie Catcher!

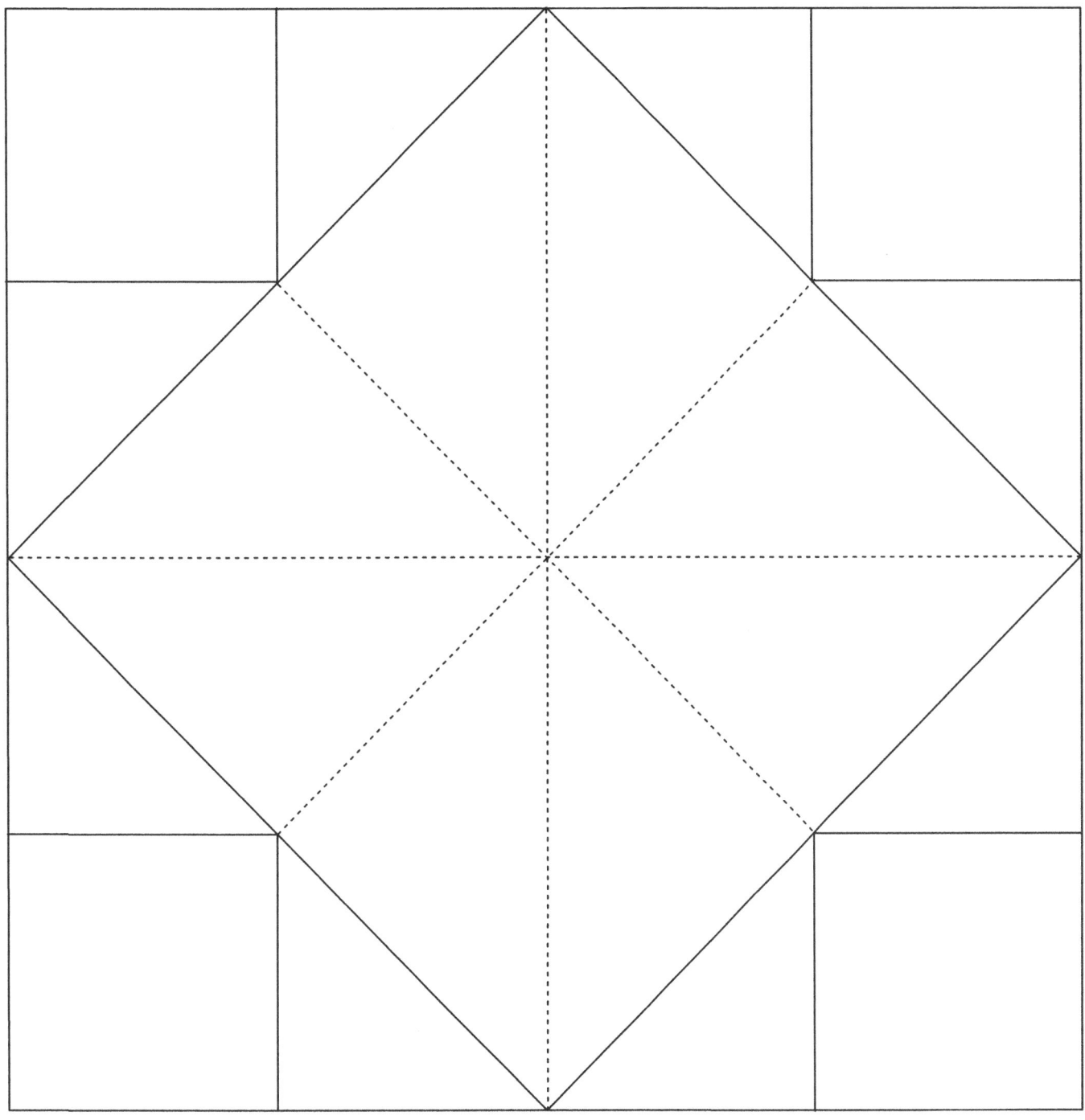

YOUR COOTIE CATCHER

Invent Your Own Cootie Catcher!

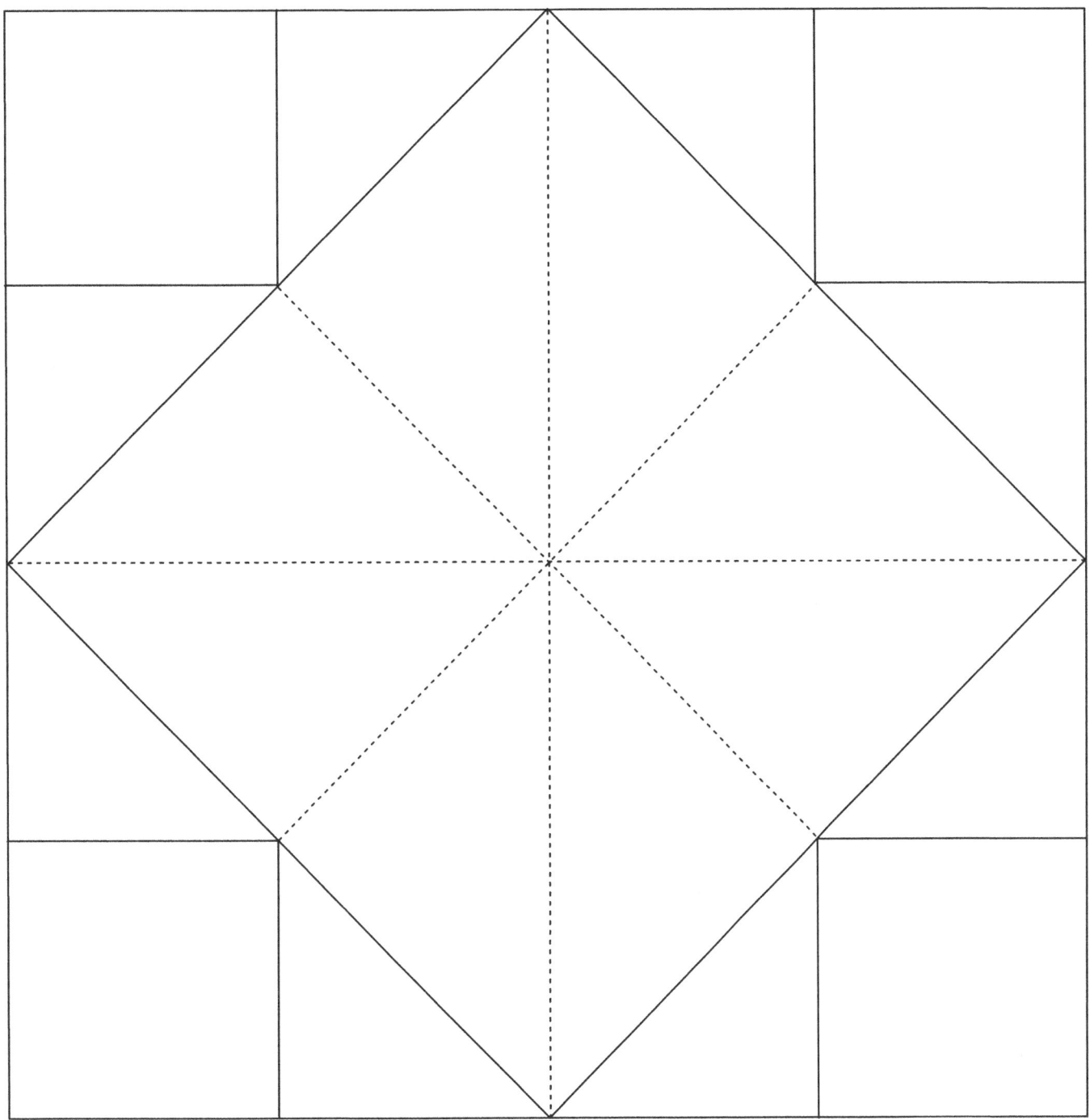

SECRET PICTURE

Do you have a super secret picture or message that you need to give to somebody? Here is the way spies do it!

DRAW A SECRET PICTURE OR MESSAGE ON A WHITE PIECE OF PAPER WITH A WHITE CRAYON. IT WILL LOOK LIKE IT IS BLANK.

THEN YOUR FRIEND CAN VIEW THE SECRET PICTURE BY DRAWING OVER IT WITH A WATER-BASED MARKER OR WATERCOLOR PAINTS

ROLL-A-DOODLE GAME

Let this game of chance predict your next drawing!

 **1.** Either find a dice or fold the paper dice template (on the next page).

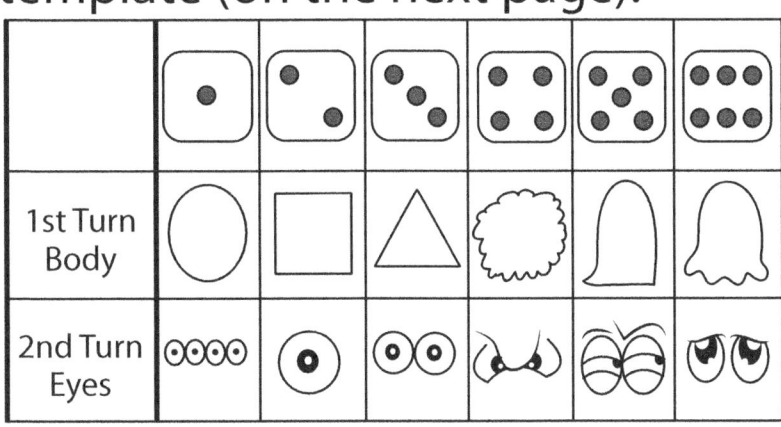

 **2.** Go to the turn that you are on ... so, for example, if you are on your first turn, then go to "1st Turn" on the first column.

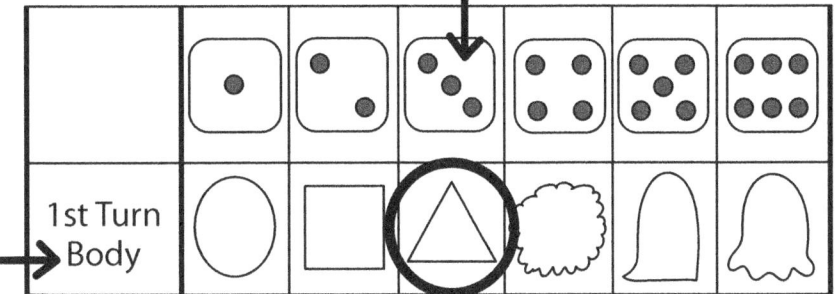

3. Roll the dice. Look for the number on the dice and match it to the dice pictured in the first row. If you are on the first turn, and you rolled a 3 on the dice, then you would draw a triangle shape (in the example above).

4. Continue on to "Turn 2" (and then the next turn, etc) until your drawing is done.

ROLL-A-DOODLE GAME

Let this game of chance predict your next drawing!

1. Either find a dice or fold the paper dice template (on the next page).

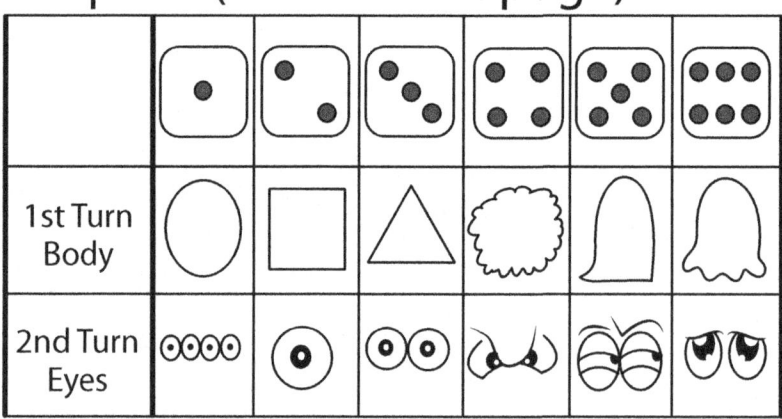

2. Go to the turn that you are on ... so, for example, if you are on your first turn, then go to "1st Turn" on the first column.

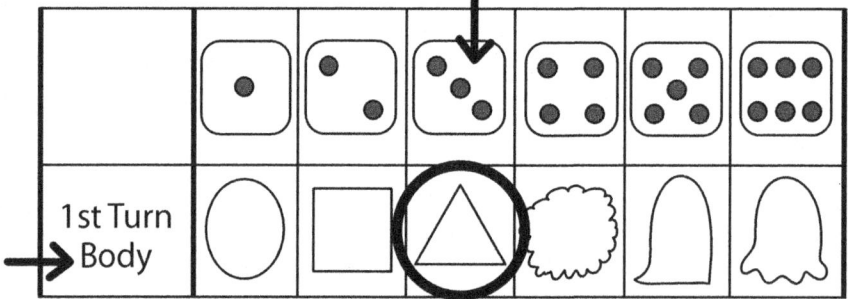

3. Roll the dice. Look for the number on the dice and match it to the dice pictured in the first row. If you are on the first turn, and you rolled a 3 on the dice, then you would draw a triangle shape (in the example above).

4. Continue on to "Turn 2" (and then the next turn, etc) until your drawing is done.

FOLD-A-DICE

Cut out the dice on the solid lines. Fold on the dotted lines. Glue or tape dice together with the tabs.

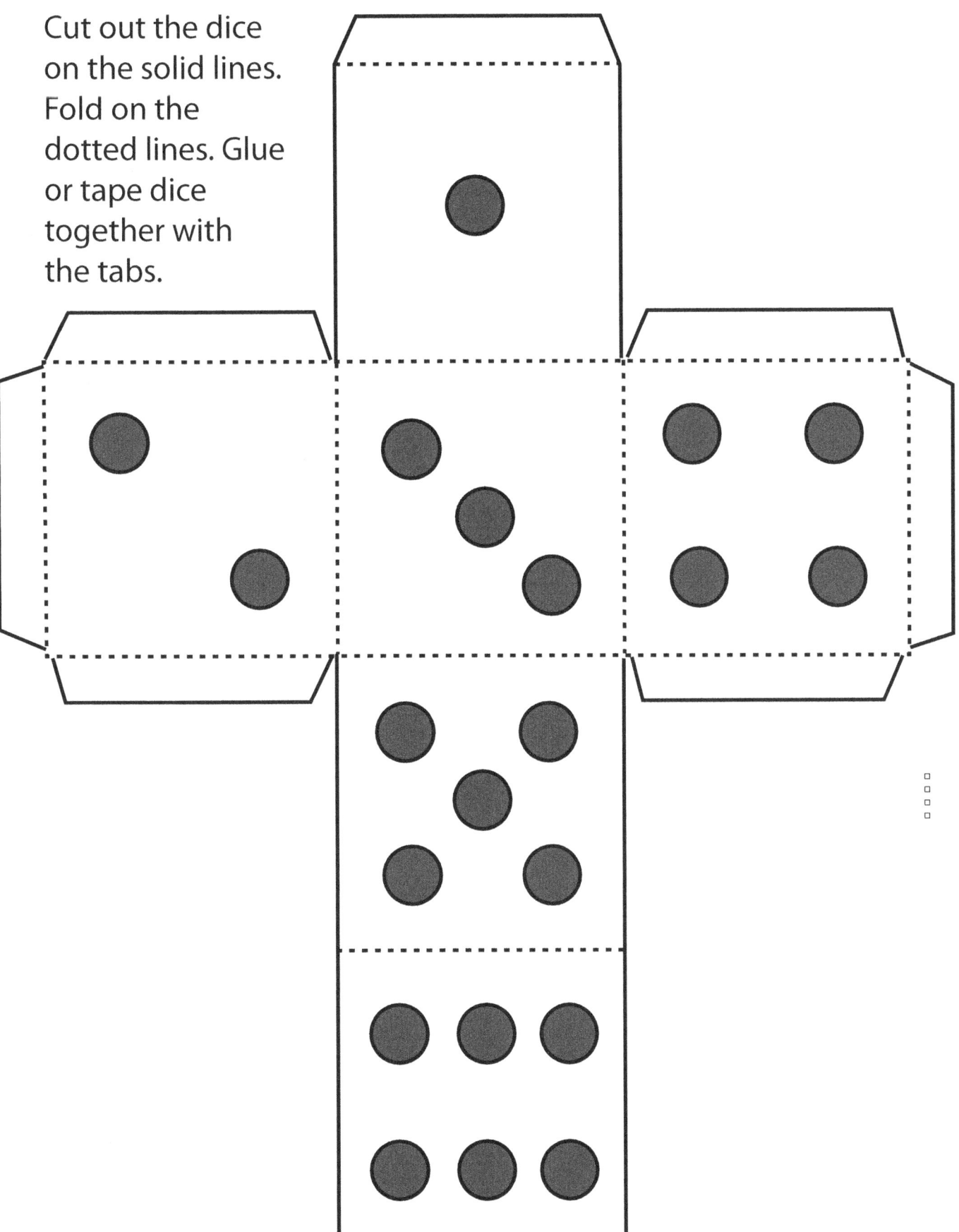

ROLL-A-CREATURE

	⚀	⚁	⚂	⚃	⚄	⚅
1st Turn Body	oval	square	triangle	fluffy blob	tombstone	ghost
2nd Turn Eyes	four small eyes	single eye	two circle eyes	angry eyes	bushy-brow eyes	looking-up eyes
3rd Turn Mouth	toothy grin	fangs	tongue out	gritted teeth	oval mouth	squiggle with fang
4th Turn Nose	no nose	circle	oval	pig snout	trunk	triangle nostrils
5th Turn Arms	stubby arms	bat wings	skeleton arms	pin arms	furry paws	clawed arms
6th Turn Legs	no feet	feet with toes	chicken feet	boots	tentacles	squiggle legs

ROLL-A-BUG GAME

	⚀	⚁	⚂	⚃	⚄	⚅
1st Turn Body	○	○○	○○○	(fluffy blob)	semicircle	peanut shape
2nd Turn Eyes	○○○○	◉	◎◎	angry eyes	glasses	cartoon eyes
3rd Turn Mouth	sharp teeth	fangs	tongue out	grid teeth	triangle teeth	antenna mouth
4th Turn Nose	no nose	○	oval	V	curved snout	nostrils
5th Turn Arms	butterfly wings	bat wings	bone arms	chevron legs	fuzzy legs	scalloped wings
6th Turn Extras	no extras	antennae	curly antennae	stripes	spots	stinger

ROLL-A-SCENE

	⚀	⚁	⚂	⚃	⚄	⚅
1st Turn Background	hills	clouds	waves	mountains	sunrise	sky/clouds
2nd Turn Plants	flower	tree	palm tree	cactus	pine tree	triangle tree
3rd Turn People	hiker	pirate	diver	police officer	chef	clown
4th Turn Things	rocket	house	UFO	sailboat	car	city
5th Turn Animals	bird	snake	dog	cow	fish	mouse
6th Turn Extras	ant	elf	monster	robot	wizard	gorilla

CLOTHESPIN PROMPT

Use the boring clothespin picture (on the next page) to start your imagination churning. Below is an example drawing...but imagine up your own picture!

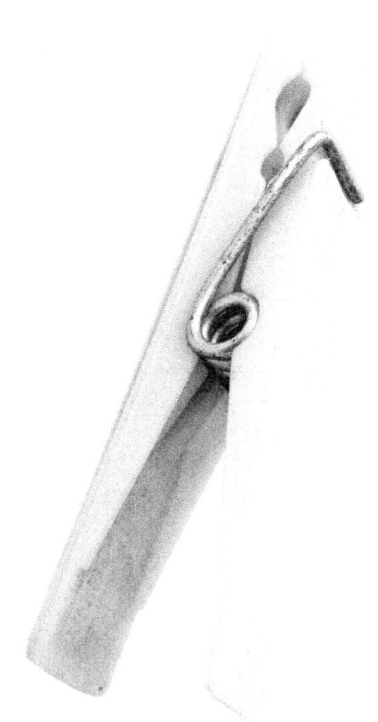

WORD SEARCH DRAWINGS

Write down the first 10 words that you find in the following word search. Then, if you dare, draw a picture using all of those words. There is a spot on the next page to draw your words.

E E A E G A B R A G F E N C E
N A I C I S U M Y R S T U V S
G R E L C G B N A U R N C A G
O E K R H L T M O E I H X P P
R A R R O A E H S C I O A E U
F P V I C S N E O L P I M S T
T E G I O S D R L H N K U R G
E N A T L E N S O T C L U O A
B C R S A S I N I O J C C H R
A I D I T O E N L E K R A C A
H L E T E D G B W S S L V U G
P N N R N T T E K N A L B D E
L I E A S E L Y E N M I H C L
A L H O C R T E N T R E E S M
E S O N Y S S E C N I R P N R

FOUND WORDS:

WORD SEARCH DRAWINGS

Write down the first 10 words that you find in the following word search. Then, if you dare, draw a picture using all of those words. There is a spot on the next page to draw your words.

C E T E L E V I S I O N
H S R M O U N T A I N B
A T A B L E P L A N E U
I P R E S I D E N T E N
R K R R T H E A R T U N
H G R R C U P C A K E Y
O E A S I U Q U E E N Y
K I N G Z O L L R T T G
N A A Z R E F T Y T T G
E T L I G H I P P O N O
R E P A R C S Y K S D D
E A B L O K I T T Y N S

FOUND WORDS:

WORD SEARCH DRAWINGS

Write down the first 10 words that you find in the following word search. Then, if you dare, draw a picture using all of those words. There is a spot on the next page to draw your words.

I	E	W	R	E	H	C	A	E	T	D	A	D
M	E	G	I	R	L	N	N	E	M	O	O	N
E	O	M	O	N	E	Y	V	E	K	A	C	M
C	C	M	R	F	D	A	N	C	S	D	T	Y
A	R	A	I	O	W	O	Y	A	O	E	C	O
R	S	S	B	O	T	O	W	L	K	W	A	B
D	H	E	R	I	B	A	P	C	A	I	P	S
S	N	C	K	W	N	H	O	N	I	Z	T	H
E	I	D	O	A	I	R	A	S	S	A	A	I
M	A	C	L	N	C	E	S	G	S	R	I	R
I	C	A	I	T	C	N	N	G	T	D	N	T
I	M	R	I	O	T	T	A	E	A	L	C	A
P	A	A	O	V	A	N	G	P	R	L	U	D

FOUND WORDS:

DRAW A COOL S

This 3-dimensional letter "S" shape is a lot of fun to doodle when you are bored. I've been drawing it since I was 8 years old.

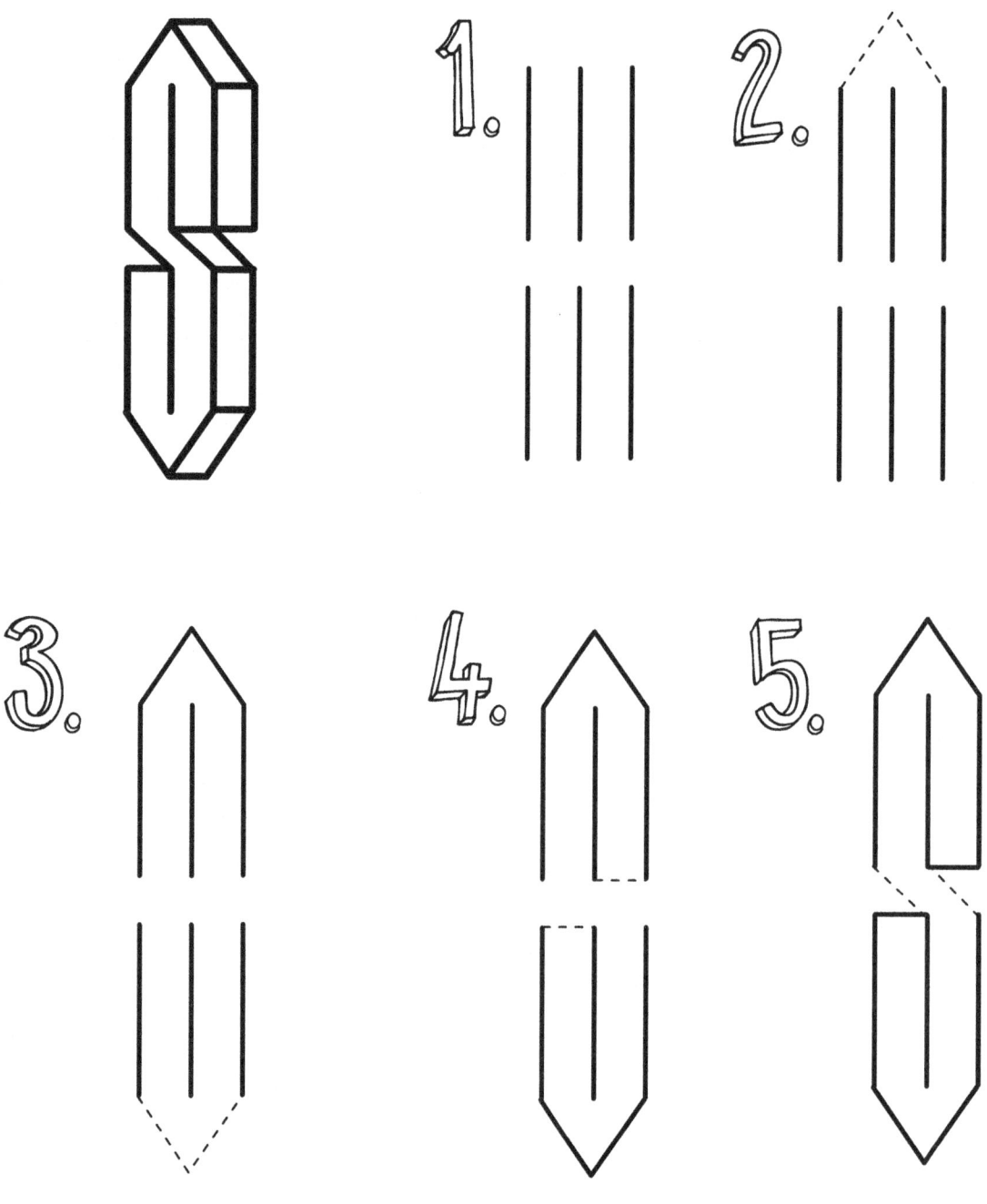

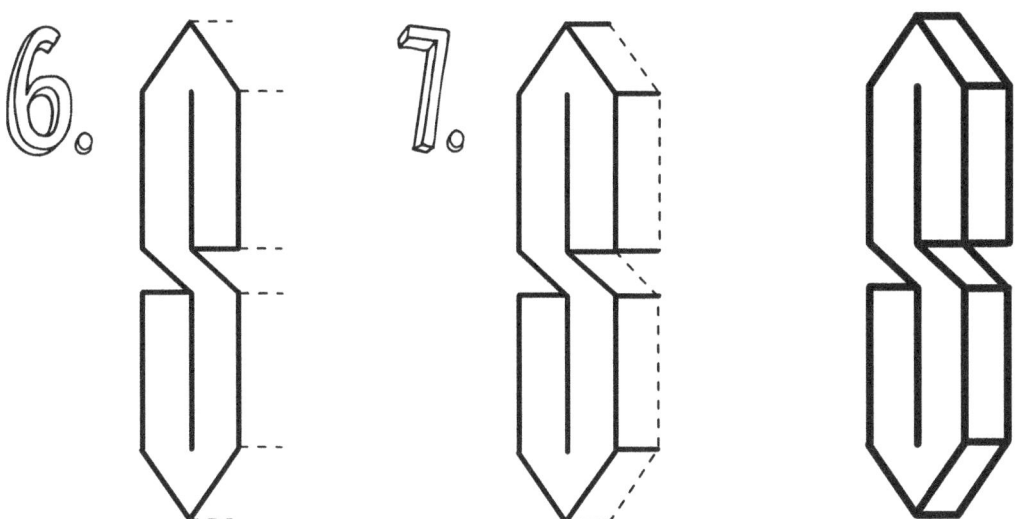

⬇ NOW YOU TRY ⬇

DRAW LETTER P BIRD

Here is a cute drawing lesson for turning a letter "P" into a bird peeping out of a tree.

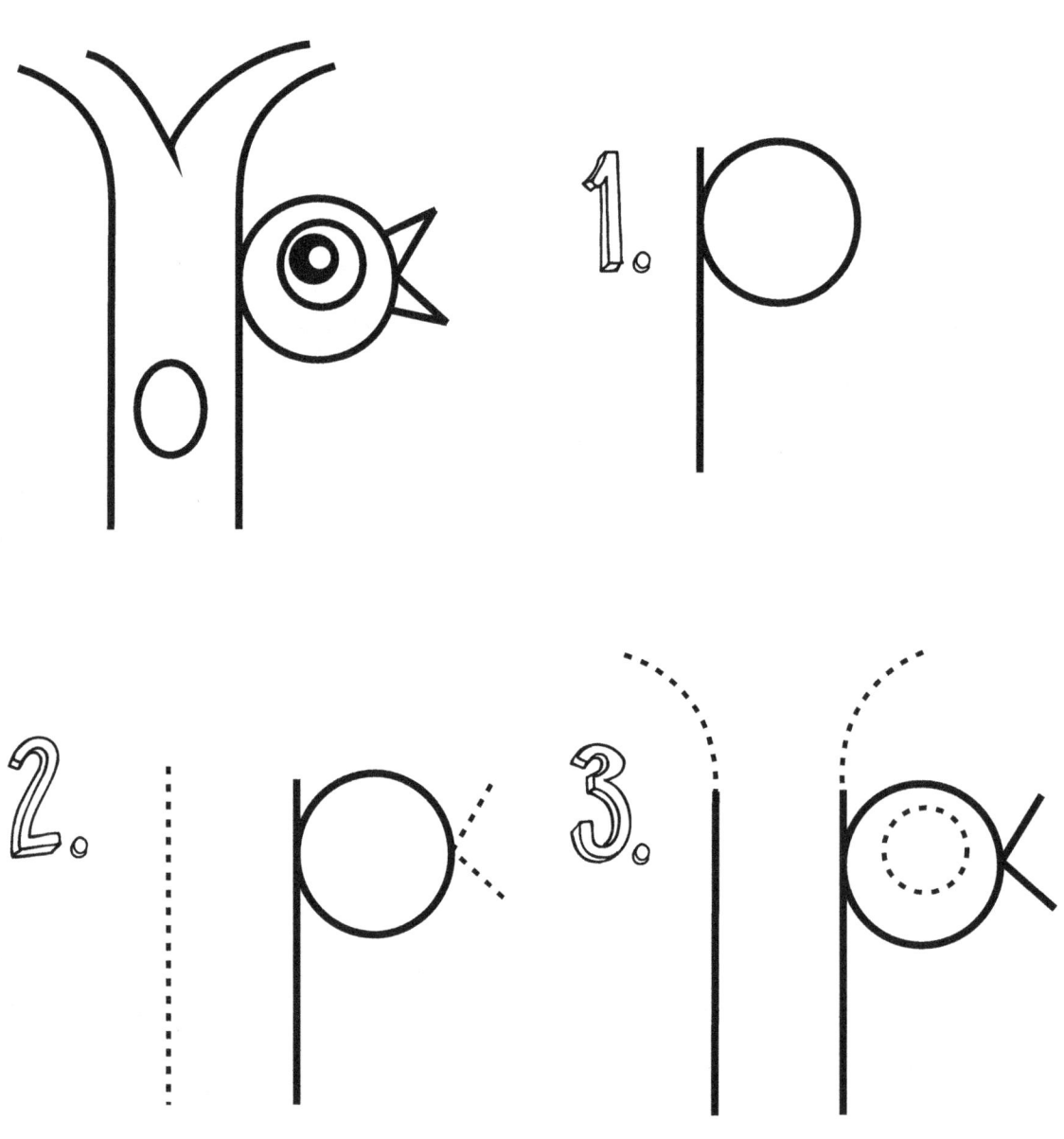

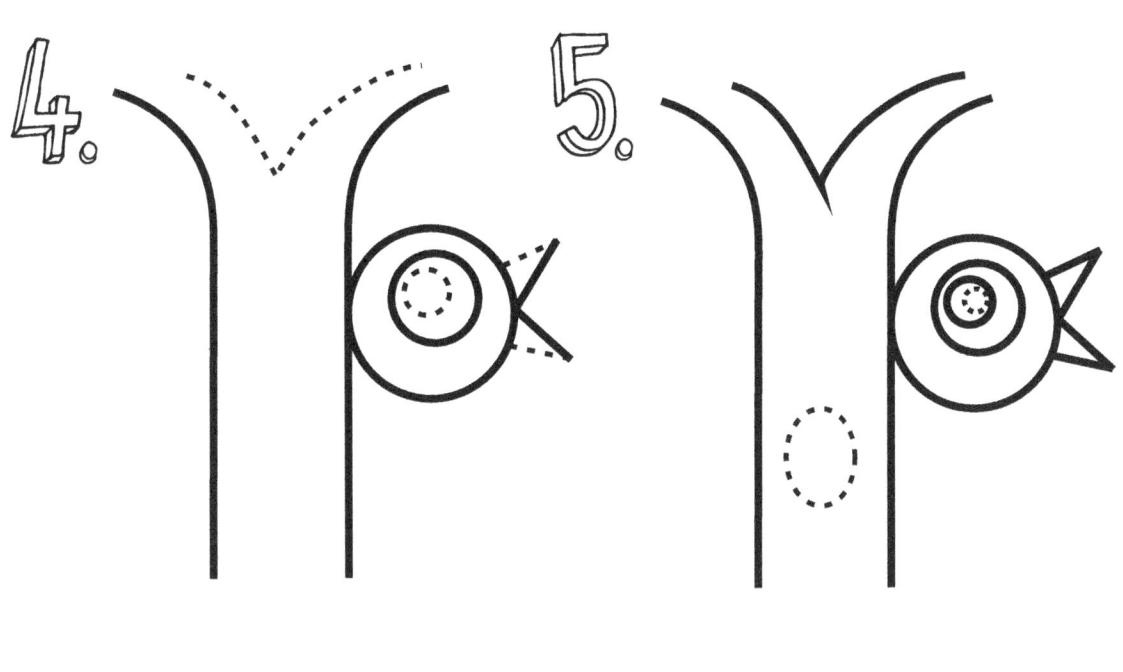

NOW YOU TRY

LETTER NUMBER DOODLES

Now you invent some letter and number drawings!

#8 Snowman

Letter E Robot

Letter A Witch

LETTER NUMBER DOODLES

Now you invent some letter and number drawings!

Letter B Butterfly

Letter F Building

Letter H House

LETTER NUMBER DOODLES

Now you invent some letter and number drawings!

Letter L Lightning

Letter M Crocodile

Letter O Face

LETTER NUMBER DOODLES

Now you invent some letter and number drawings!

Letter P Face with Tongue Out

Letter R Crocodile

Letter S Snake

LETTER NUMBER DOODLES

Now you invent some letter and number drawings!

Letter U Bird in Nest

Letter V Ice Cream Cone

Letter W Mountains

LETTER NUMBER DOODLES

Now you invent some letter and number drawings!

Letter Y Cat (Hint: Use the "Y" as the Nose)

Number 3 Heart

Number 6 Eyes

ONE LINE DRAWING

This is more of a challenge than a game...but a challenge that almost every artist has tried. In art school they make you do this challenge when you are learning how to draw. They also make you do this with your eyes closed...so if you want an extra challenge, try this as well.

Try to draw without lifting your pencil off of the paper. You can try to draw anything, but here are some ideas : house, dog, cat, girl, boy, vase, flower, horse, goat, car, truck, etc. It is hard to do, but it is fun attempting to draw things this way!

ONE LINE DRAWING

Try the one-line-drawing challenge on this page.

ONE LINE DRAWING

Try the one-line-drawing challenge on this page.

3D HAND

Here is a trick to make it look like you drew a 3-dimensional hand!

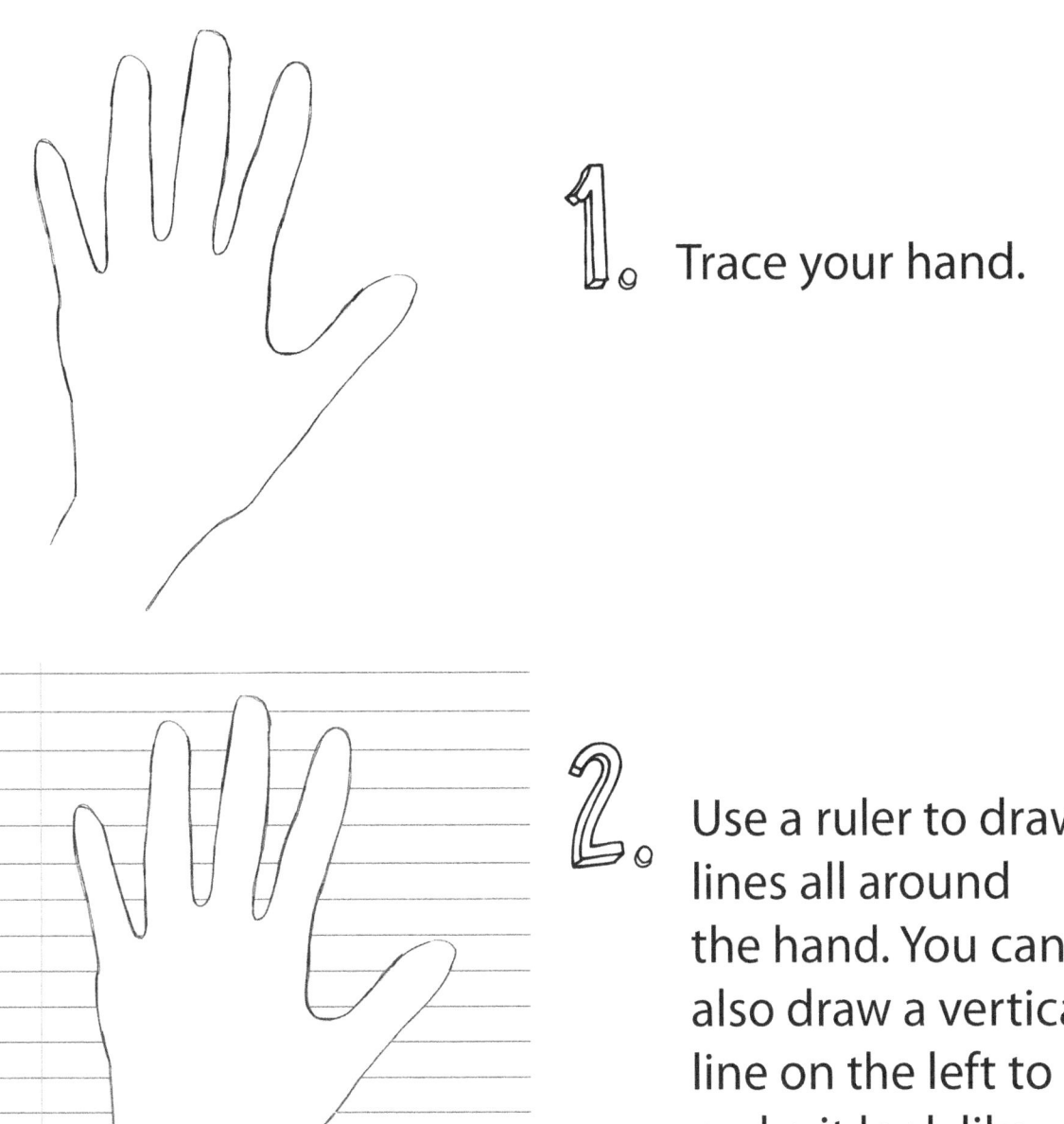

1. Trace your hand.

2. Use a ruler to draw lines all around the hand. You can also draw a vertical line on the left to make it look like notebook paper.

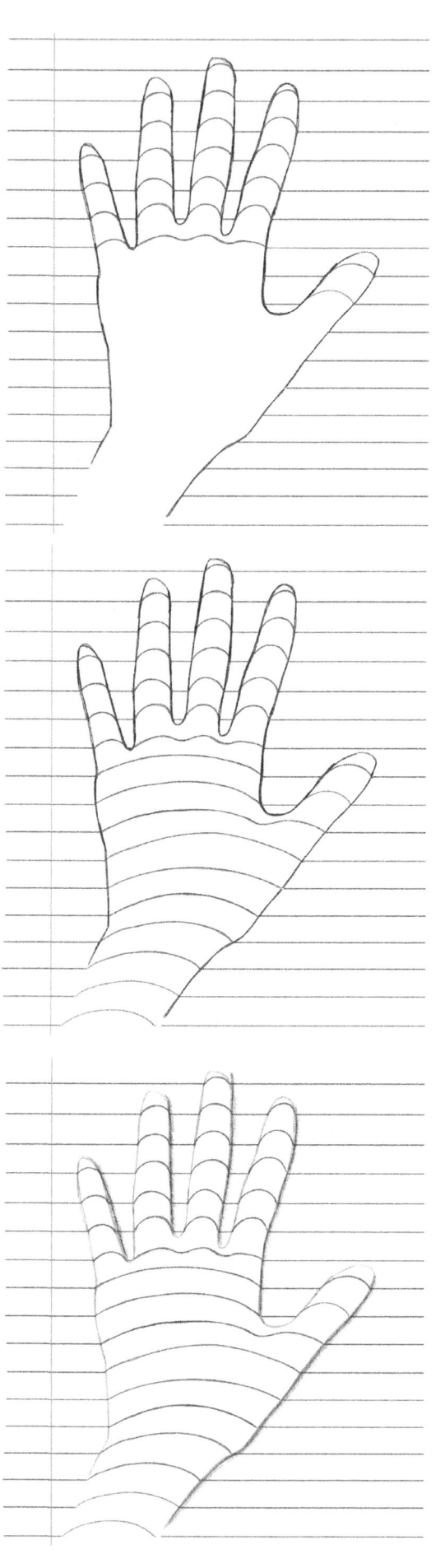

3. Draw curved lines around fingers to make it look like the lines are bulging over the fingers.

4. Draw curved lines over the rest of the hand.

5. Add shadow to the right side of fingers.

DRAW THE 3D HAND

SYMMETRICAL GAME

Here is a challenging game to play between two friends. It is fun, but only some people will be able to do it...so don't get frustrated!

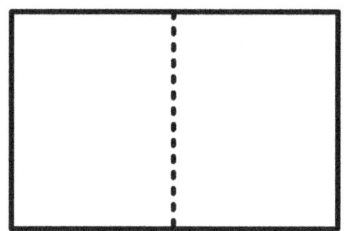 **1.** Fold a page in half. Each player chooses a side.

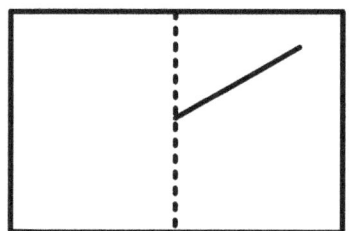 **2.** The first player draws a line on his side of the page.

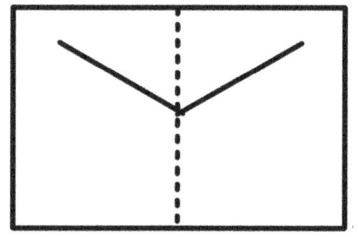 **3.** The second player draws a mirror image of the line that was drawn by the first player.

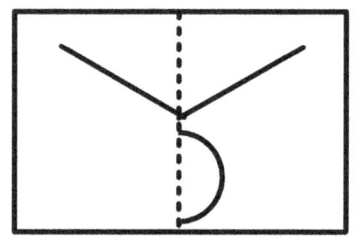 **4.** The first player draws another line on his side of the page.

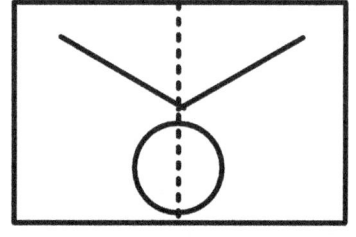 **5.** The second player draws a mirror image of the line that was drawn by the first player.

SYMMETRICAL GAME

This goes on and on and on and on and on and on until either the 2nd player makes a mistake or there is no more room on the page. There are no winners or losers in this game...it is all in good fun!

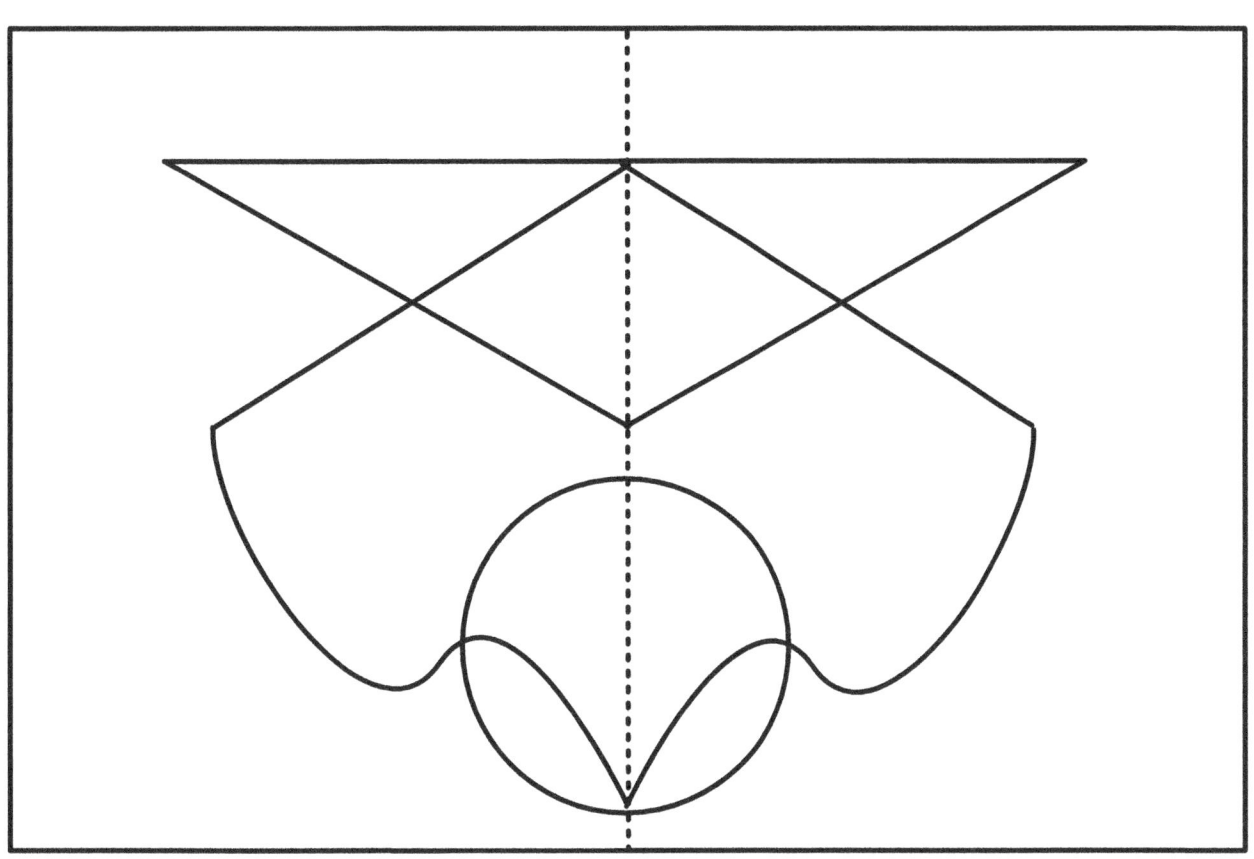

MAKE CUBES PUZZLES

This is a great puzzle game that you can customize to make into your very own art creation. This is a bit of work to fold up, but it is worth it. Have fun!

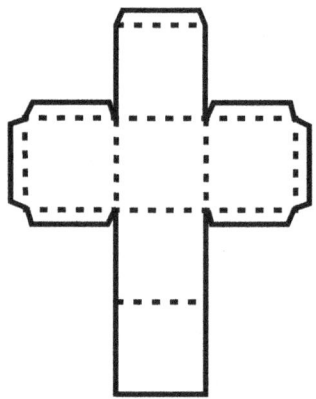

1. Fold up all of the cubes (there are 9 of them).

2. Line up all 9 of the cubes to form a large square. Draw a picture using all 9 squares.

3. Then turn all the cubes over so that there are blank sides again. Line them all up so the 9 cubes form a large square again. Draw another picture using all 9 squares. Do this until all blank sides are gone. You will now have 6 puzzles! Have fun!

FOLD-A-CUBE

Cut out the cube on the solid lines. Fold on the dotted lines. Glue or tape cube together with the tabs.

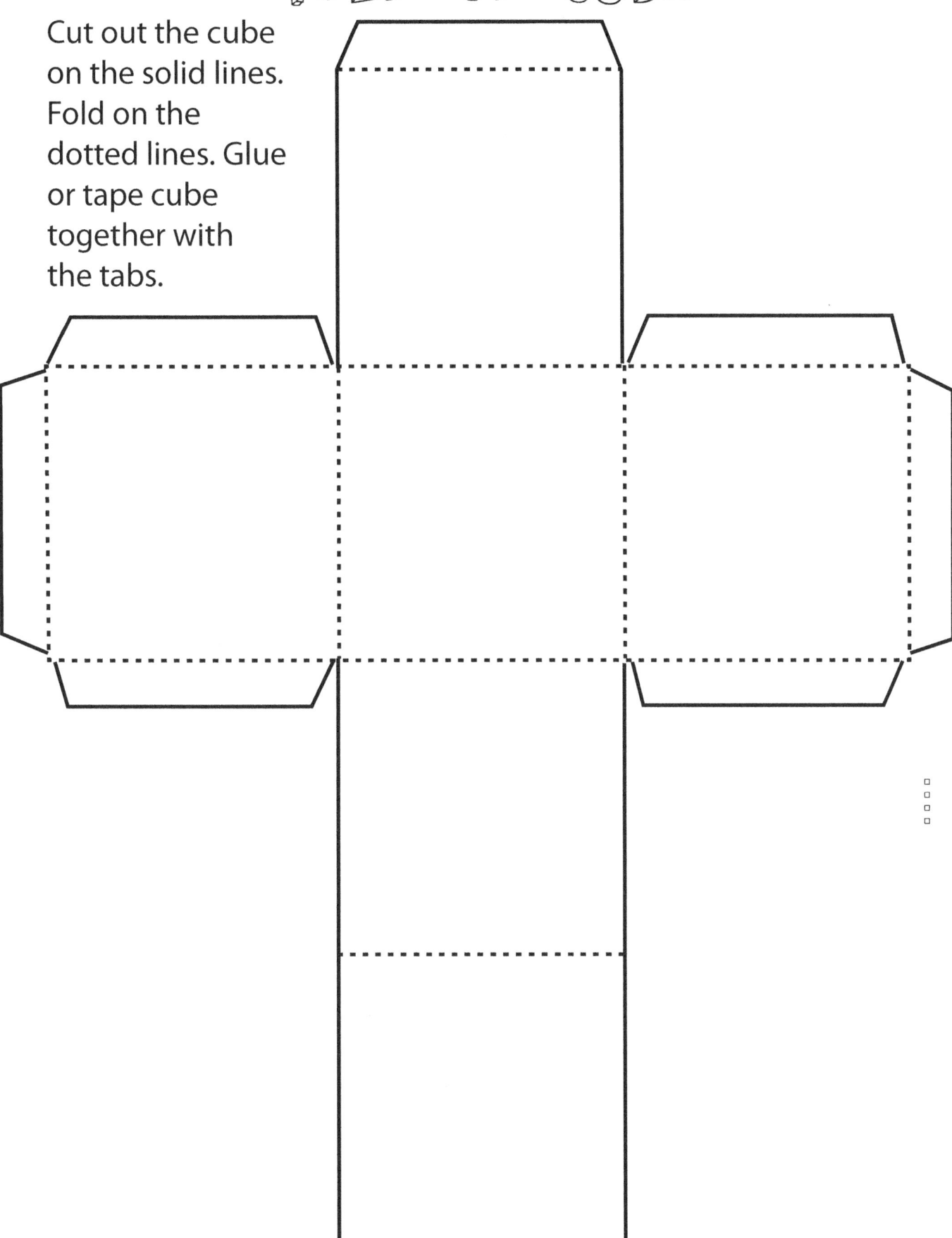

FOLD-A-CUBE

Cut out the cube on the solid lines. Fold on the dotted lines. Glue or tape cube together with the tabs.

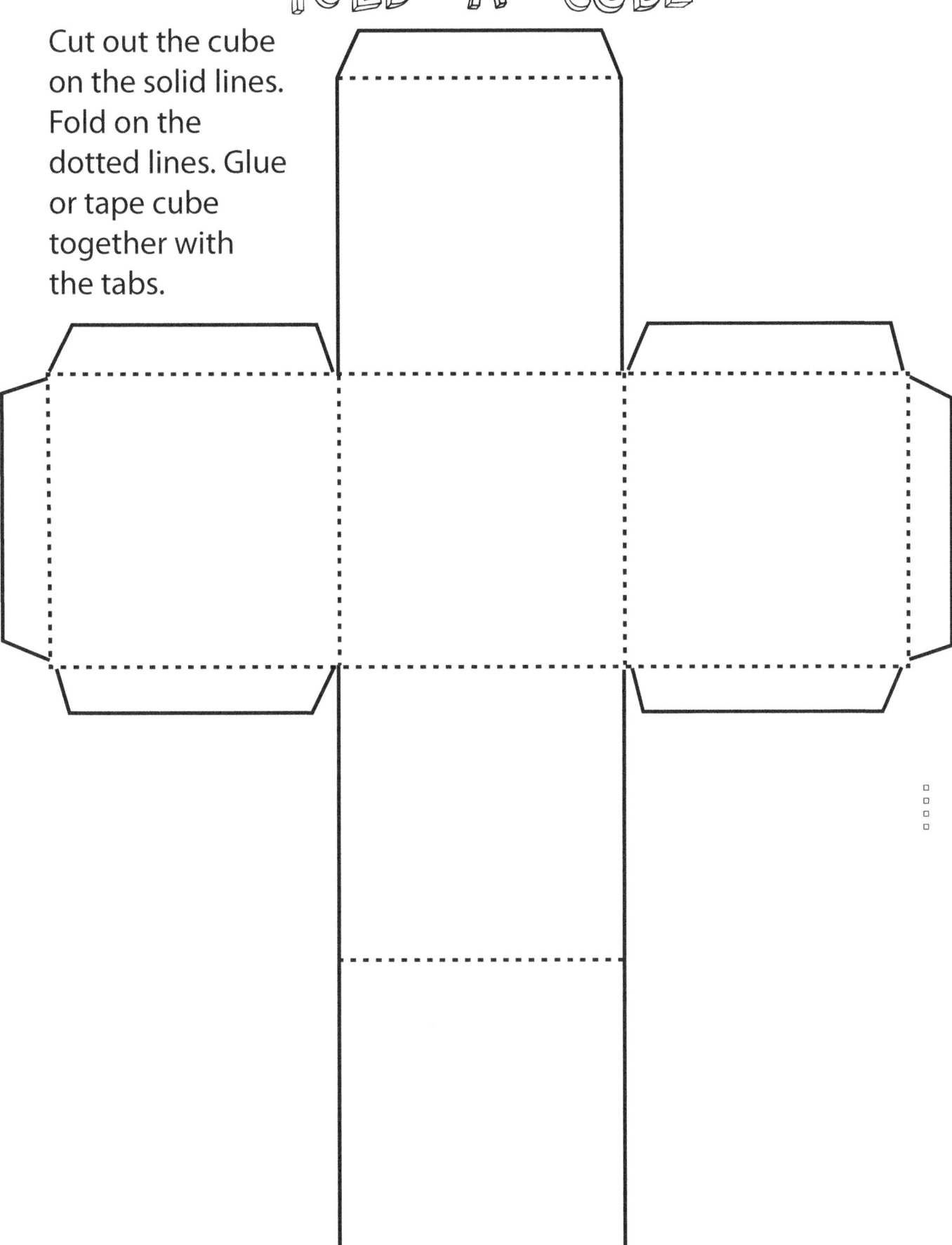

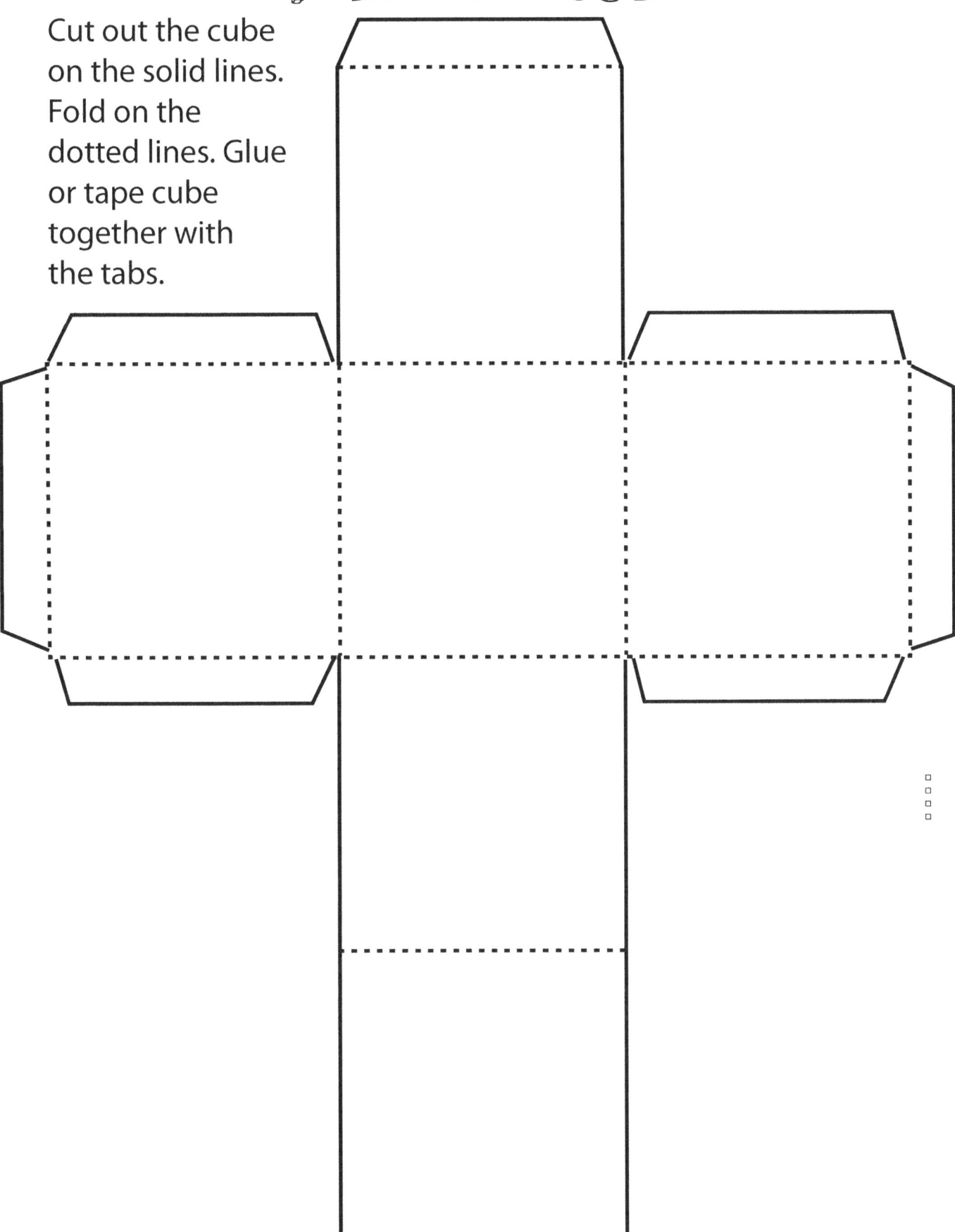

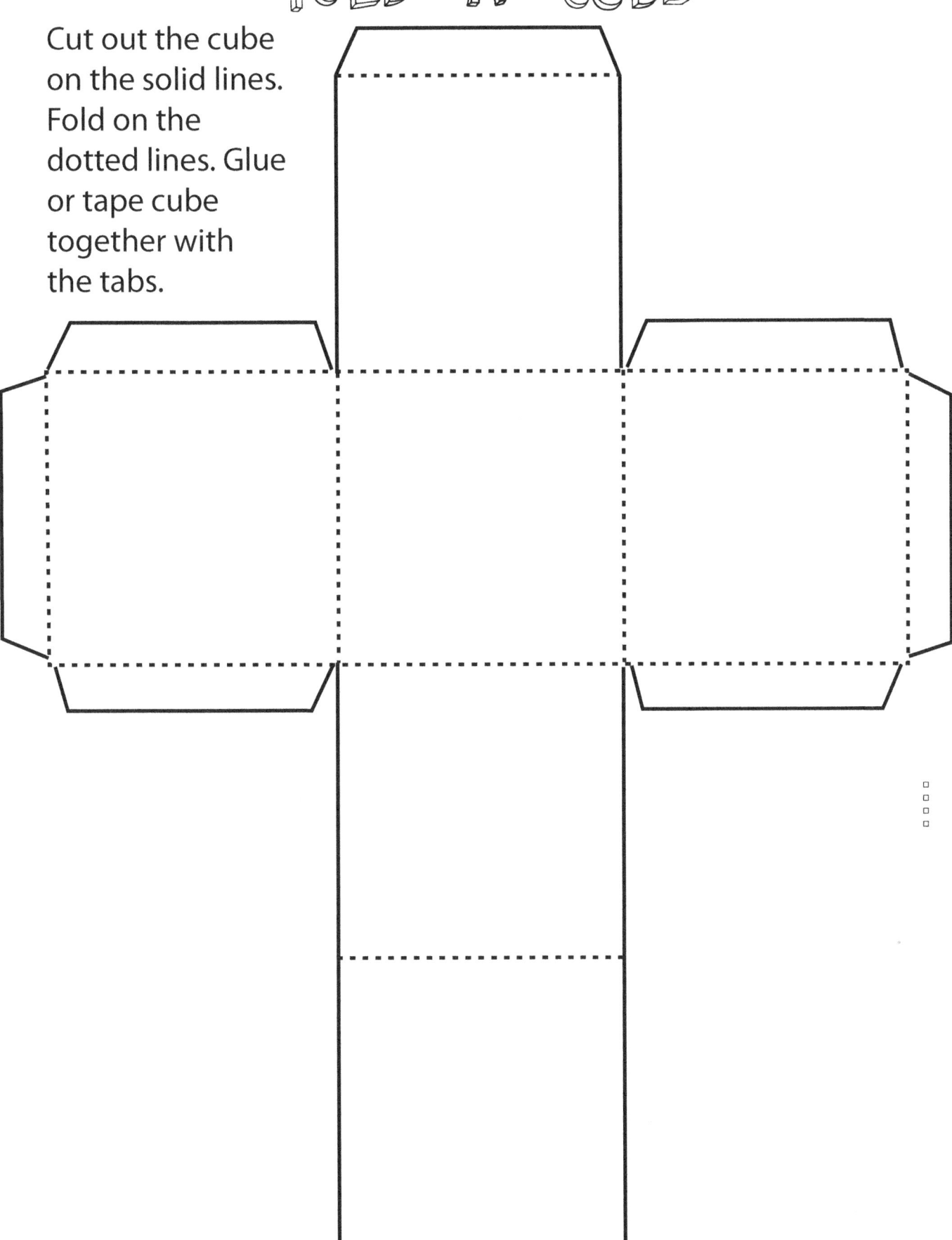

FOLD-A-CUBE

Cut out the cube on the solid lines. Fold on the dotted lines. Glue or tape cube together with the tabs.

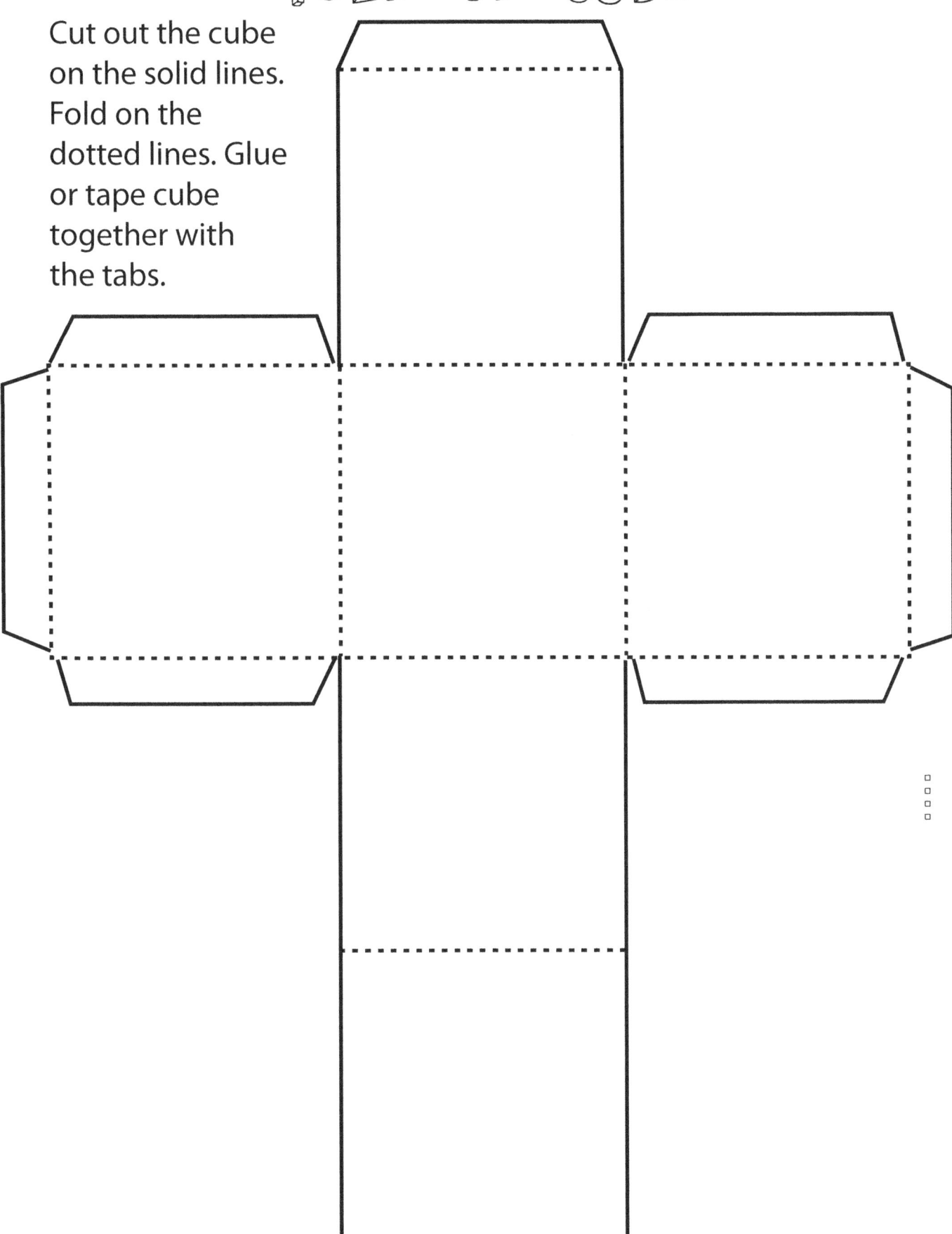

FOLD-A-CUBE

Cut out the cube on the solid lines. Fold on the dotted lines. Glue or tape cube together with the tabs.

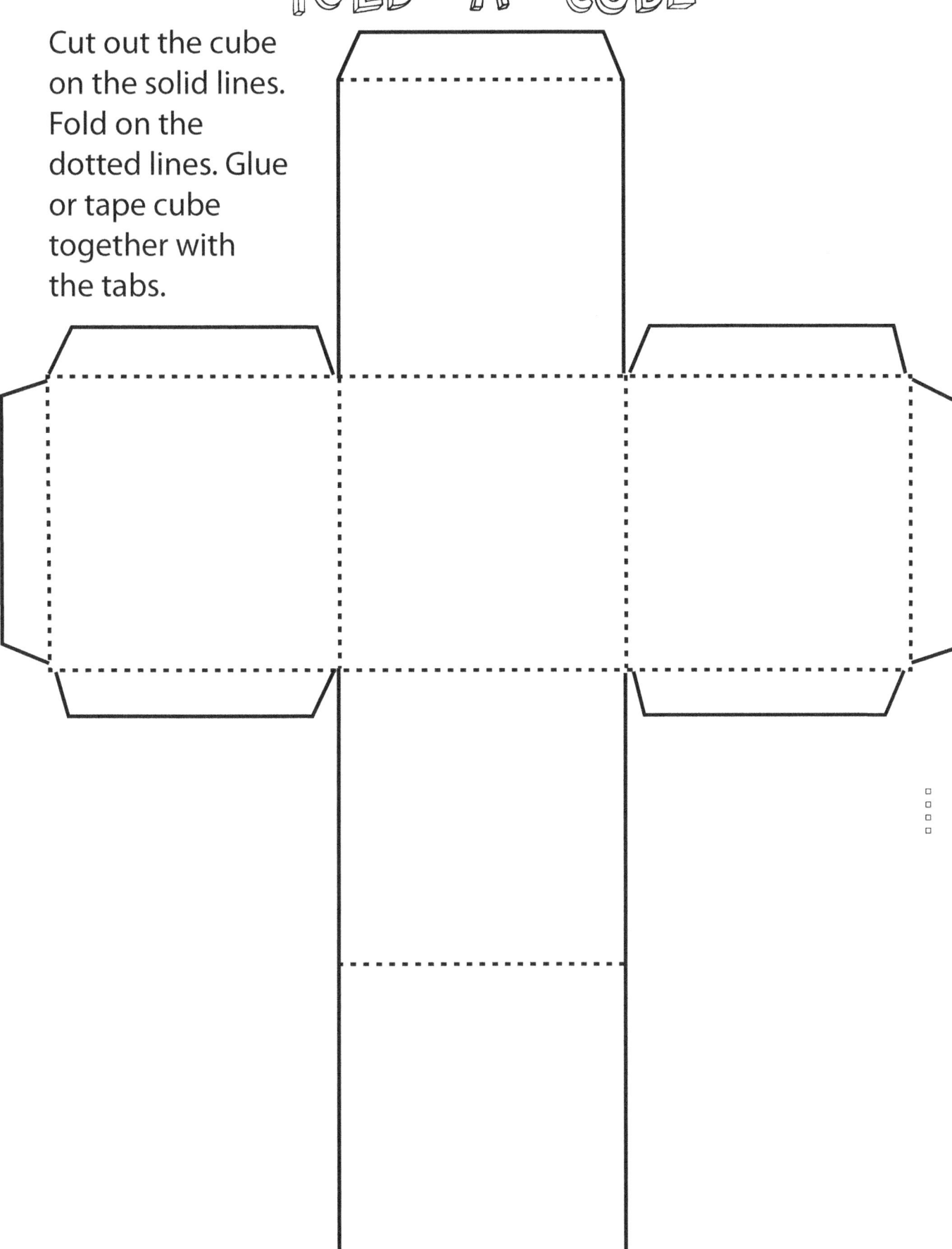

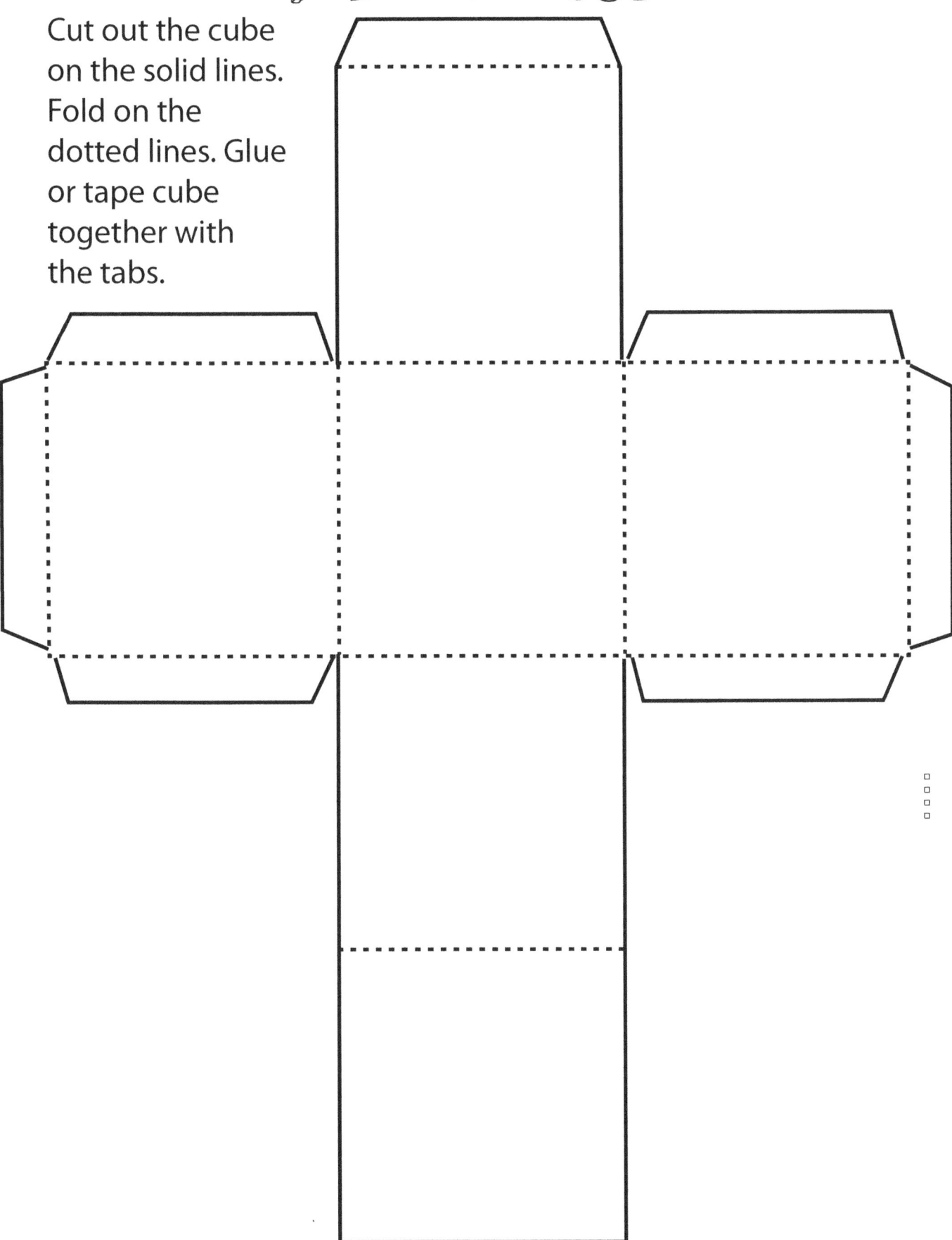

FOLD-A-CUBE

Cut out the cube on the solid lines. Fold on the dotted lines. Glue or tape cube together with the tabs.

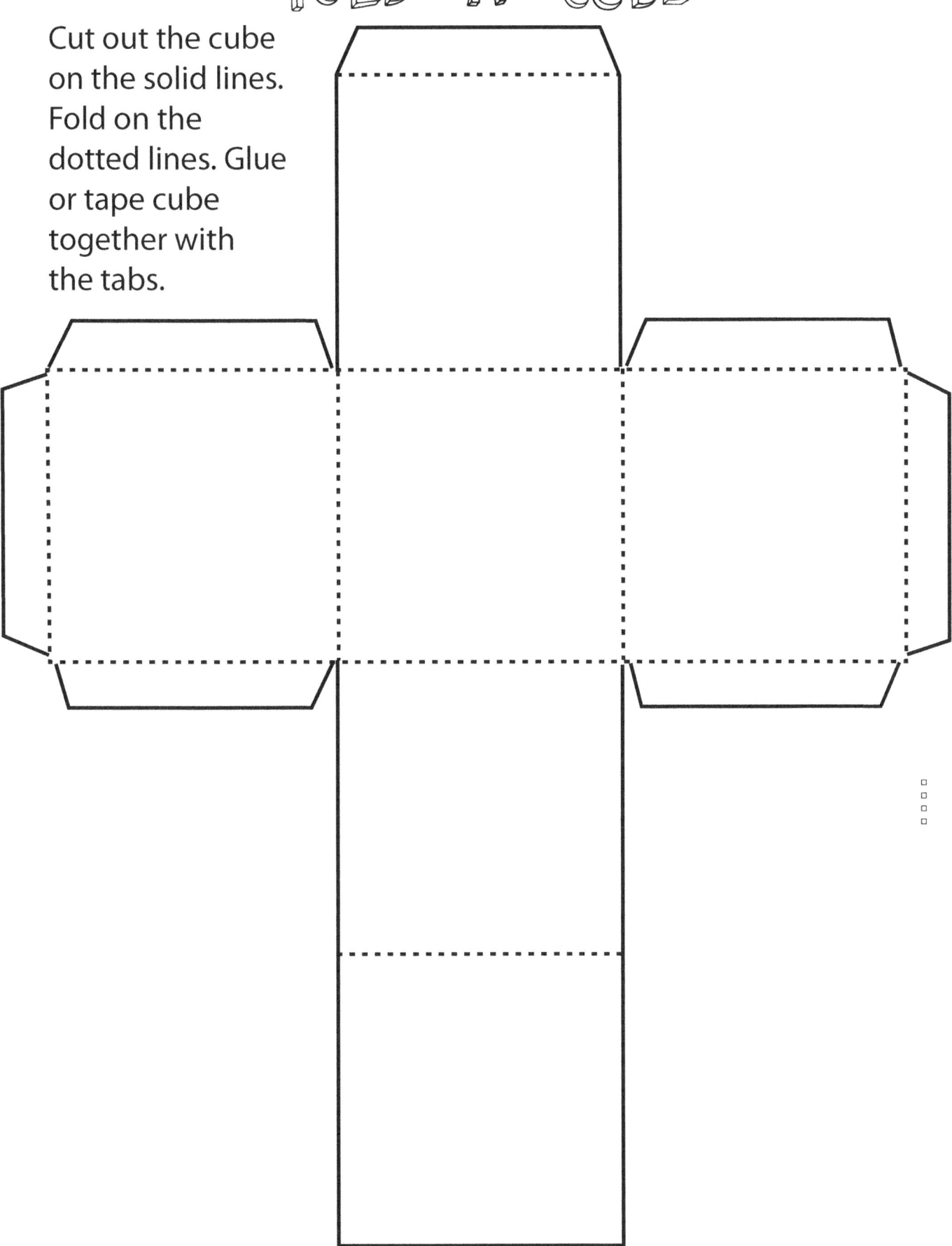

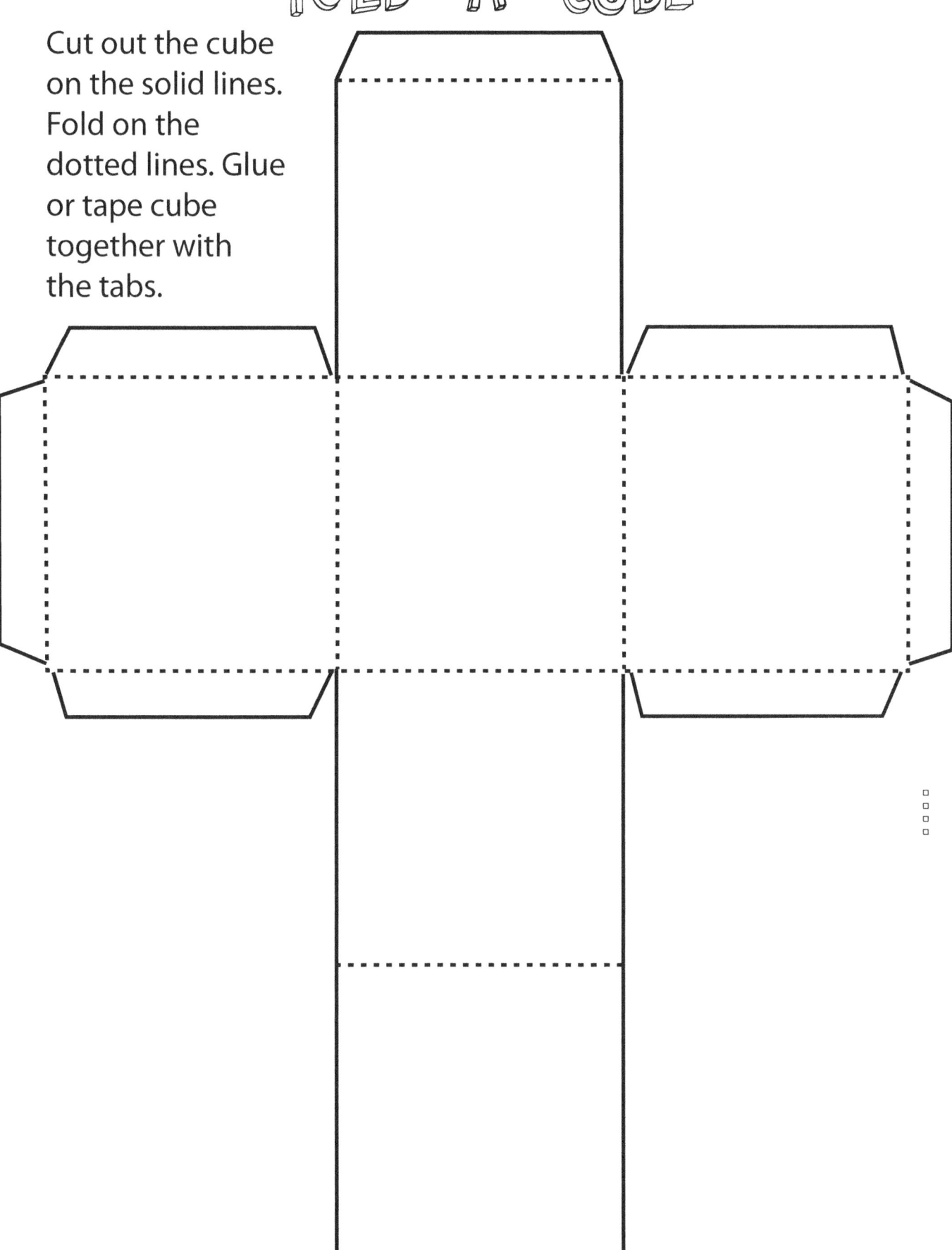

DRAW A WORD FROG

This is a really cool drawing tutorial. I will show you how to draw a cartoon frog from the word "frog"!!!

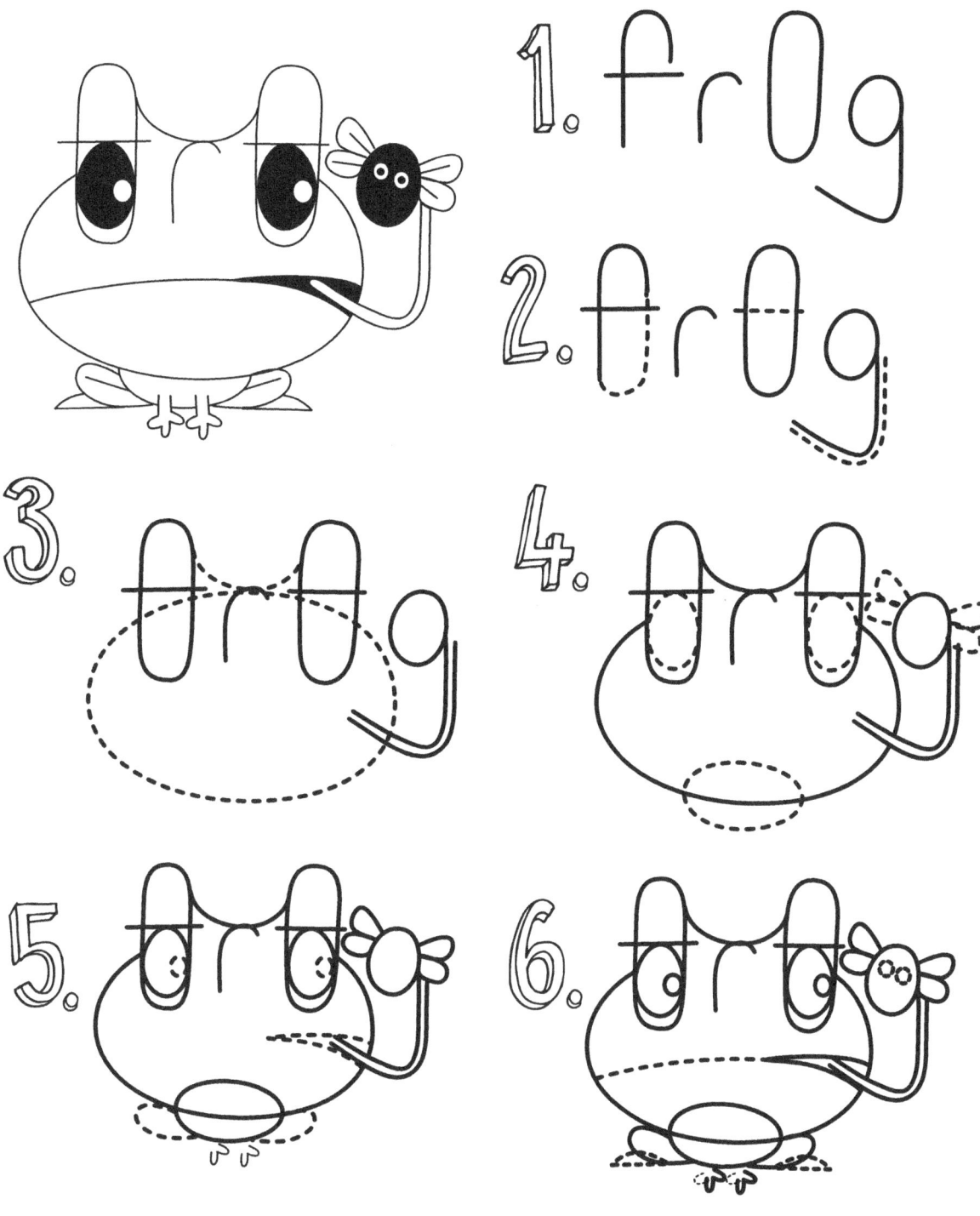

7.

⬇ NOW YOU TRY ⬇

DRAW MISSING PARTS

We have erased parts from the 3 drawings below. Look at the first picture to see what we erased...then draw the missing parts.

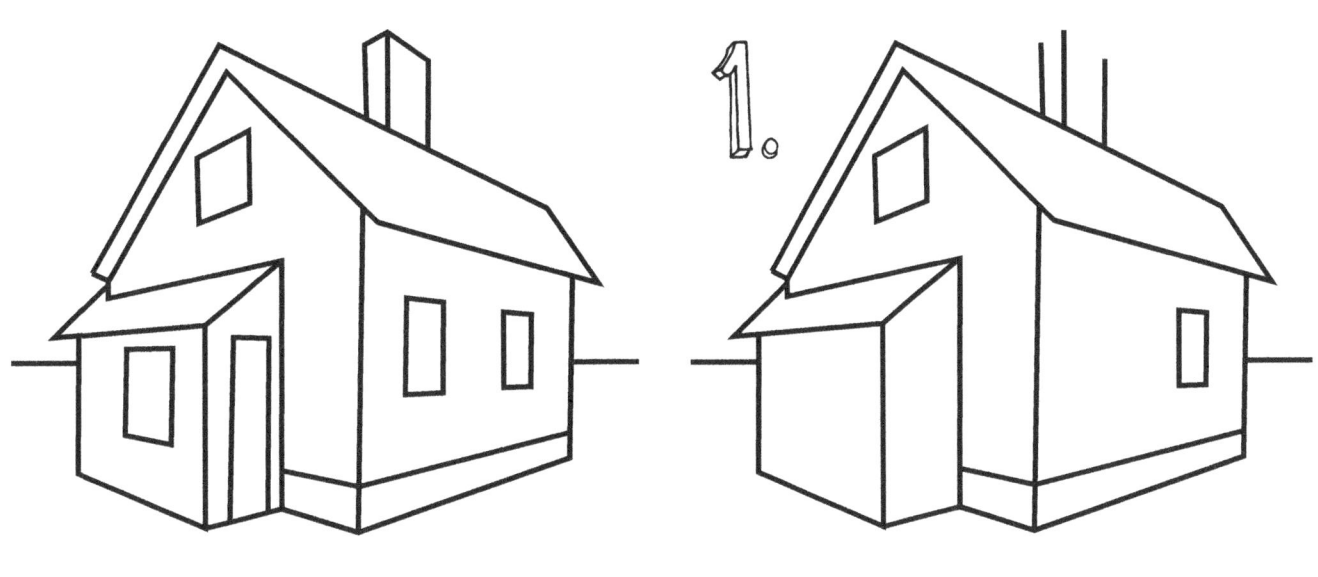

DRAW MISSING PARTS

We have erased parts from the 4 drawings below. Look at the first picture to see what we erased...then draw the missing parts.

DRAW MISSING PARTS

We have erased parts from the 3 drawings below. Look at the first picture to see what we erased...then draw the missing parts.

DRAW MISSING PARTS

We have erased parts from the 3 drawings below. Look at the first picture to see what we erased...then draw the missing parts.

DRAW MISSING PARTS

We have erased parts from the 3 drawings below. Look at the first picture to see what we erased...then draw the missing parts.

DRAW MISSING PARTS

We have erased parts from the 3 drawings below. Look at the first picture to see what we erased...then draw the missing parts.

FINISH THE SQUIRREL

Uh Oh! Part of this squirrel has disappeared!!! Finish drawing the squirrel so he can go back to doing squirrel stuff!!

PAPERCLIP PROMPT

Use the boring paperclip picture (on the next page) to start your imagination churning. Below is an example drawing...but imagine up your own picture!

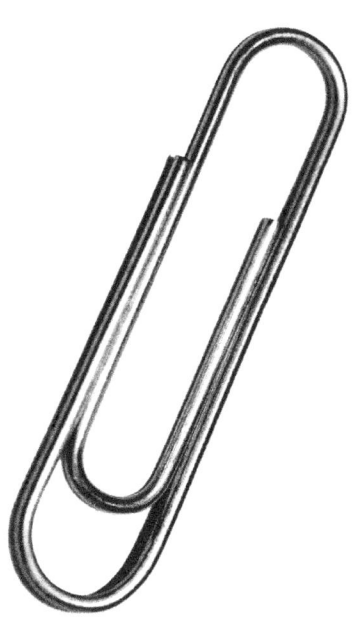

FINISH THE SHARK

Uh Oh! Part of this evil shark has disappeared!!! Finish drawing this shark so he can go back to doing evil stuff!!!

3D TEEN PIMPLES

Finish this drawing of a teenage boy or girl (you choose). Then turn the page over and give him or her disgusting pimples!!!

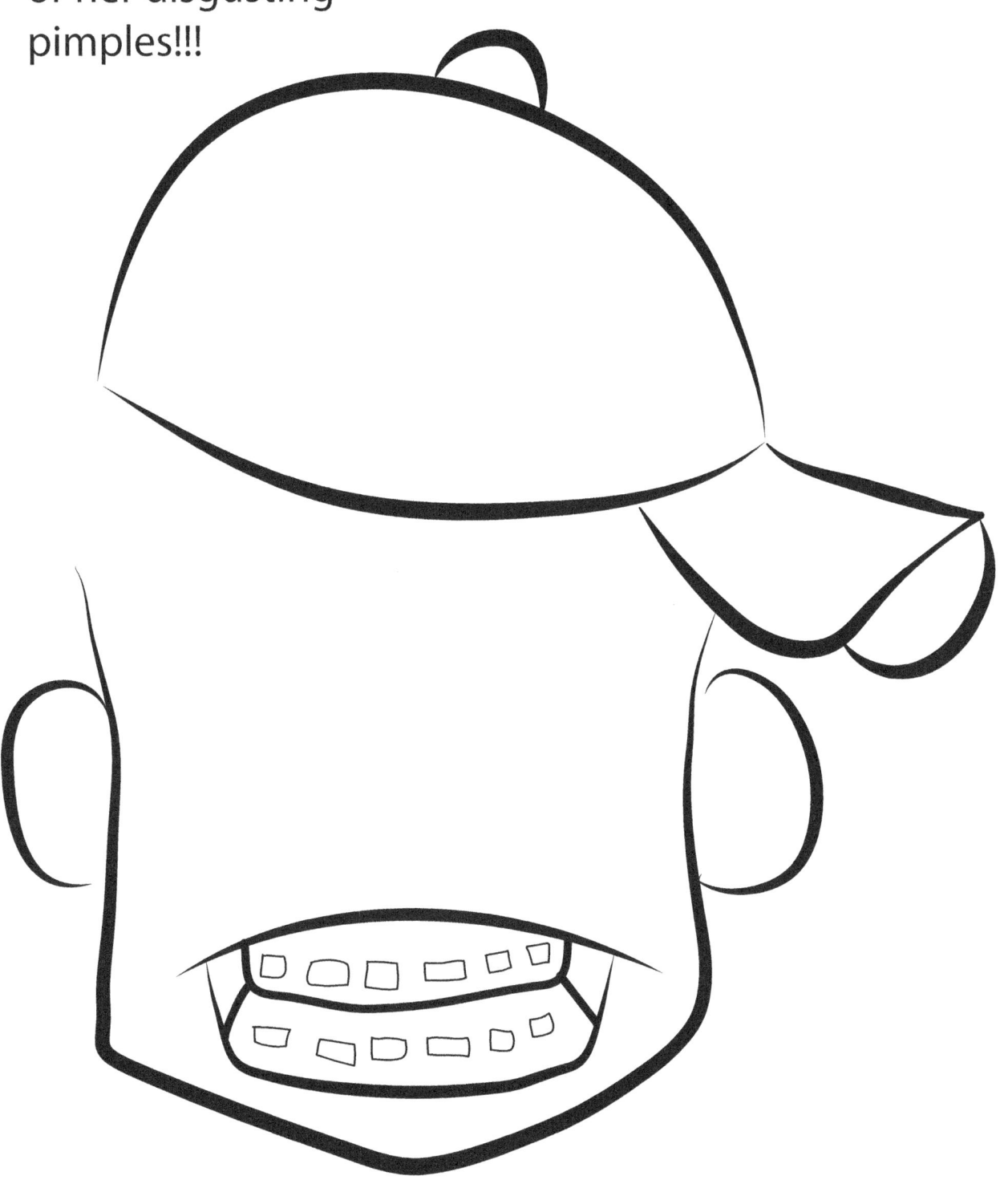

Use your pencil to poke holes behind the teen's face to make it look like pimples are popping out of the face.

FINISH THE FIGURES

What or who are these figures? Are they monsters, robots, kids, or whatever? Choose what each of these figures are and then draw them...the sillier the better!

FINISH THE SAILOR

Uh Oh! Part of this sailor has disappeared!! Draw the other part of his body before his ship-mates notice!

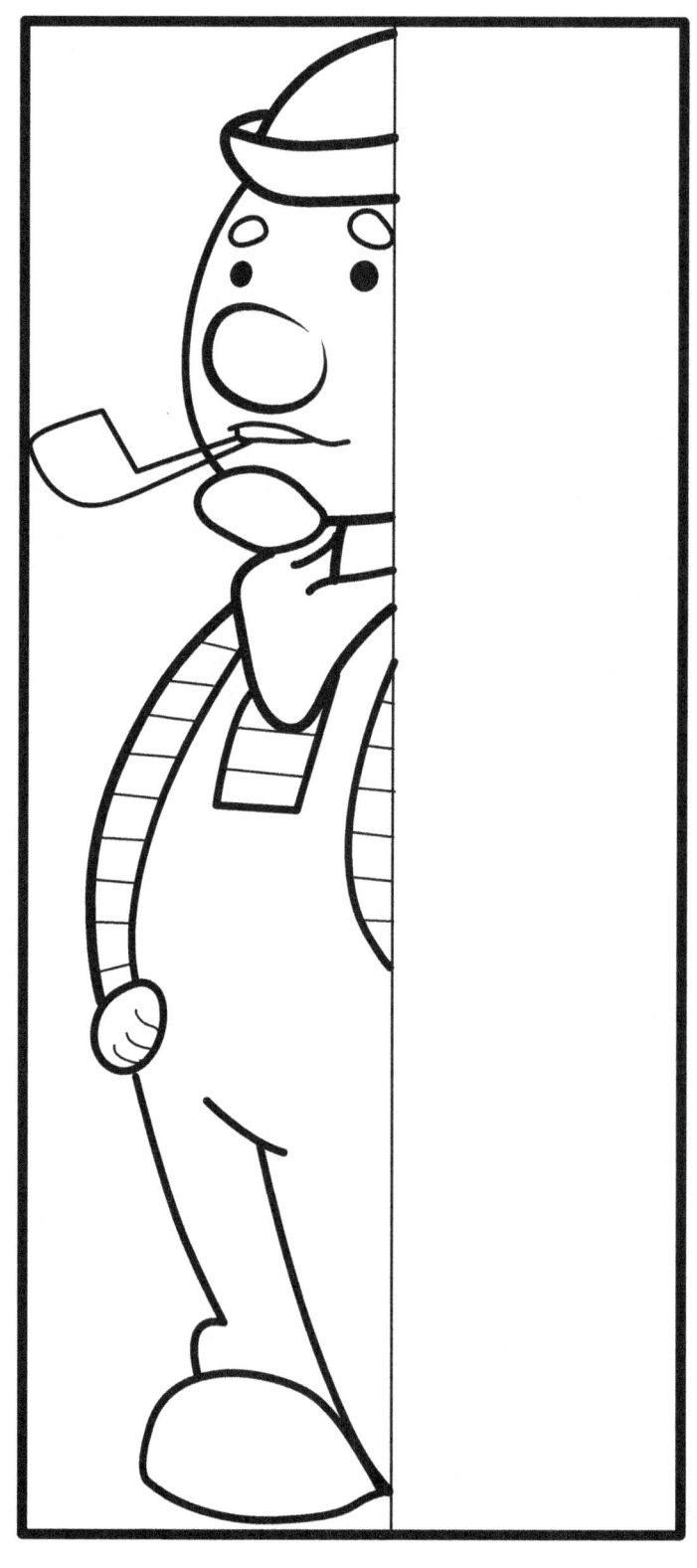

PICTURES IN THE CLOUDS

On the next few pages you will find pictures of clouds. Stare at the clouds until you see a picture...then draw the picture you see...just as I have done (Yes...that is a bird-fish). Have fun!

PAPER DOLL CHAIN

1. Cut Out the entire rectangle.
2. Fold on the lines in an accordion fold. Make sure the person is at the top when finished folding.

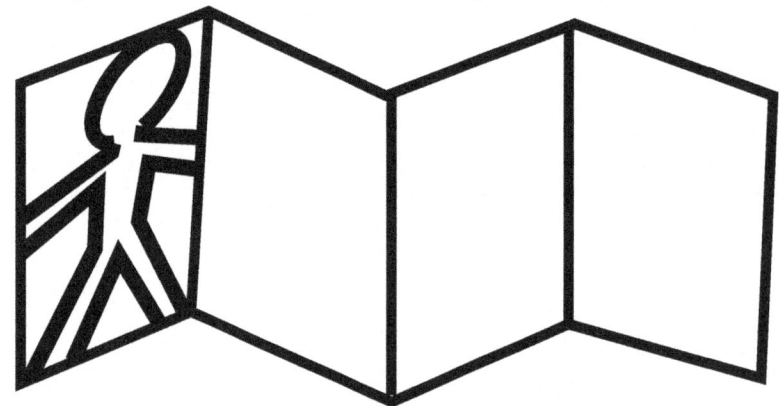

3. With the paper all folded...cut the person out on the dark lines. DO NOT CUT on the sides of the arms (where it is a dotted line).

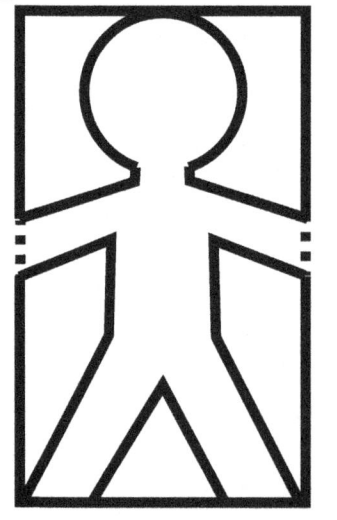

4. Now is the fun part. Draw in the faces and the clothing for each paper doll. Have fun and be creative!

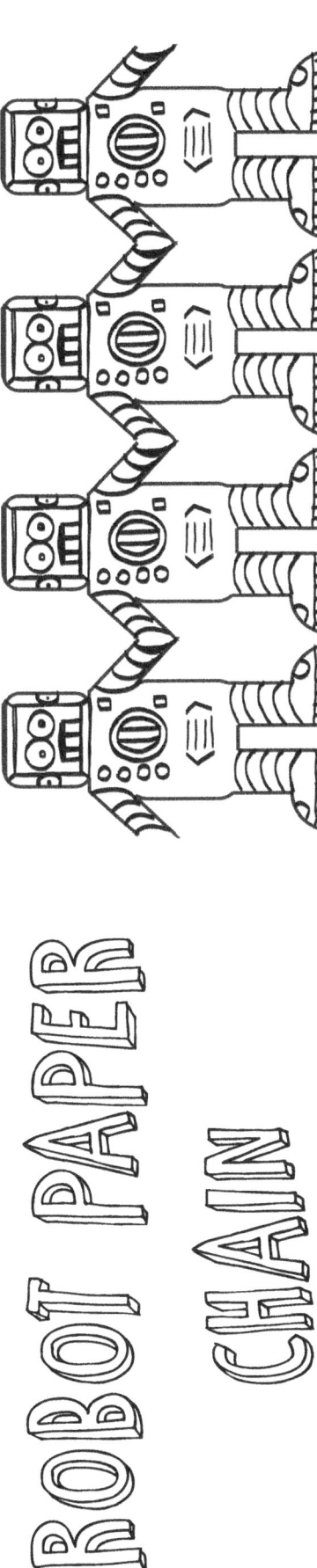

ROBOT PAPER CHAIN

REFLECTED NAME

Draw a picture that looks like your name is reflected in the water. Coolio!

USE A MARKER THAT IS STILL NEW ENOUGH THAT IT IS SOPPING WET. QUICKY WRITE YOUR NAME (CURSIVE OR PRINT) IN CENTER OF PAGE.

FOLD OVER PAGE AND PUSH DOWN SO THAT THE IMPRINT OF YOUR NAME PRINTS ON TO THE OTHER SIDE OF THE PAGE. IF YOUR NAME ONLY SHOWS UP LIGHTLY, THEN DRAW OVER YOUR NAME SO IT IS DARKER.

QUICKLY SMUDGE THE NAME THAT YOU COPIED SO THAT IT IS A BIT BLURRY. IF IT IS DRY, YOU MIGHT NEED TO USE A TINY BIT OF WATER ON A PAINT BRUSH TO SMUDGE IT. THEN DRAW A WIGGLY LINE BETWEEN BOTH NAMES. DRAW CURVY LINES AROUND NAME TO LOOK LIKE YOUR NAME IS IN THE WATER. ADD TO YOUR DRAWING...AND BE CREATIVE.

COMBO CREATURES

Here is a silly game to play with your friends (although you can play it alone on the next few pages)! A piece of paper gets passed around where each person writes down a type of animal or type of person (such as a teacher or fireman) until there are about 5 things written down. Then each player has to draw a combination of all the items that were written down. Then pass around the pictures to see who has the funniest drawing!

Bug
Cat
Dragon
Elephant
Giraffe

COMBO CREATURES

Combine 4 or 5 from the following :

Dog ... Cat ... Baby ... Bear ... Artist ... Elephant ... Fairy

COMBO CREATURES

Combine 4 or 5 from the following :
Fireman ... Giraffe ... Mouse ... Whale ... Fox ... Teacher

COMBO CREATURES

Combine 4 or 5 from the following :
Astronaut ... Rat ... Lion ... Kangaroo ... Pup ... Dancer

FUNNY CREATURE GAME

Here is a fun game that needs to be played with a friend. In this game you will make a crazy creature together. You can play it with 3 folds (head / body / feet) or with 4 folds (head / upper body / lower body / feet).

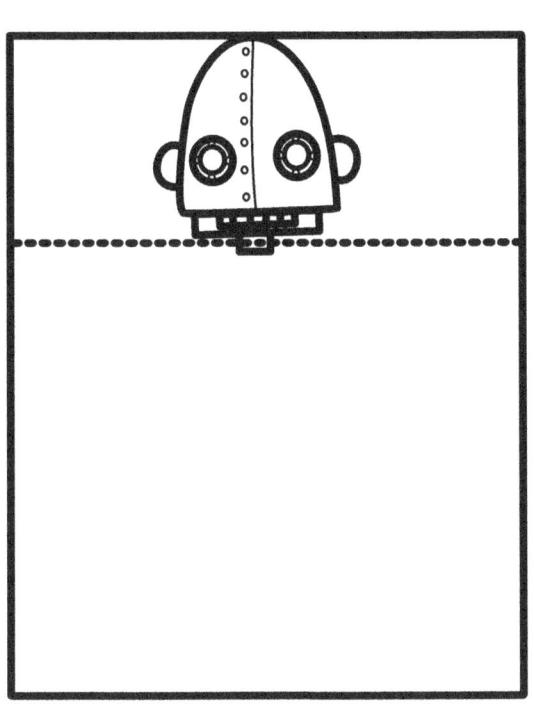

1.

The first person should draw an Animal, Person, or other Figure on the top portion of the paper...then fold the paper back. Extend the neck past the fold.

2.

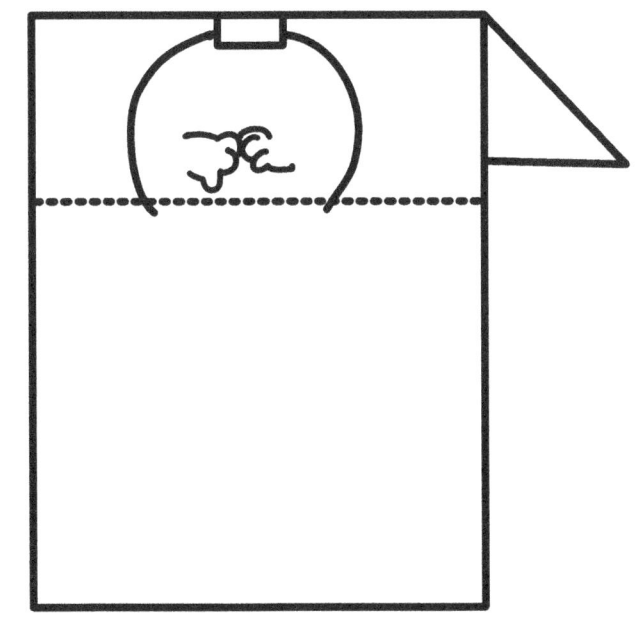

Now the second player will draw the body of a different Animal, Person, or other Figure. Then fold paper back again. Extend body a bit past the fold.

FUNNY CREATURE GAME

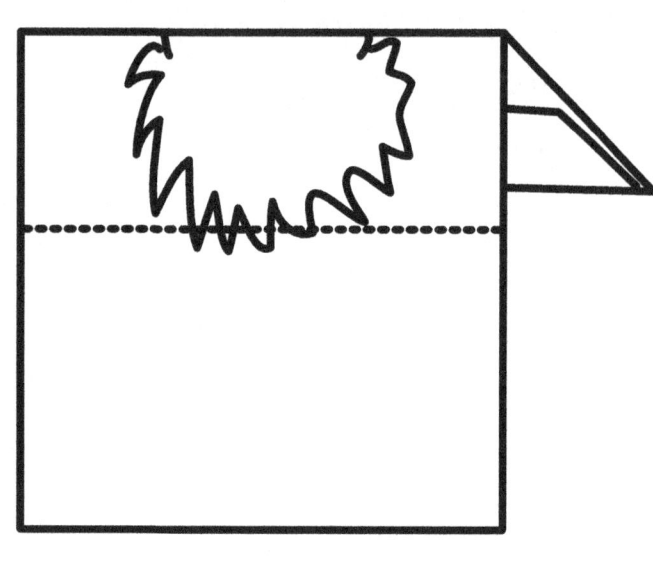

3.

Now it is the first person's turn again. Draw the lower body of a different Animal, Person, or Figure, extending it a bit past where you will fold it. Fold over the paper again.

4.

Now the second person draws the legs of a different Animal, Person, or Figure.

Now open up the paper so you can both giggle about the picture you just drew! You can play this for hours...it never gets old!

DRAWING TELEPHONE

Have you ever played telephone? It is a fun game where the first player in the circle whispers a word into the ear of the person sitting to their right. Players whisper the word to their neighbors until it reaches the last player in line. Then the first and last player compare their words to see if it was relayed correctly.

Well in Drawing Telephone, words are replaced with drawings - as you probably have guessed. Here is how to play the game:

  The first player writes down a word on a notepad

  The notebook is handed to the player to the right. This player secretly looks at the word, then turns to the next page and draws a picture of that word.

Monkey

The notebook is passed to the next person to the right. This player examines the picture and then writes down what he/she thinks the word is on the next page.

The notebook is handed to the player to the right. This player secretly looks at the word, then turns to the next page and draws a picture of that word.

Ferret

And it continues on until the last person.

Man

Compare the first word and the last picture to see if they match!

SYMMETRICAL DRAWING

Vases are symmetrical - meaning that if you cut the vase in half, both sides would be exactly the same. Draw the other halves of these vases.

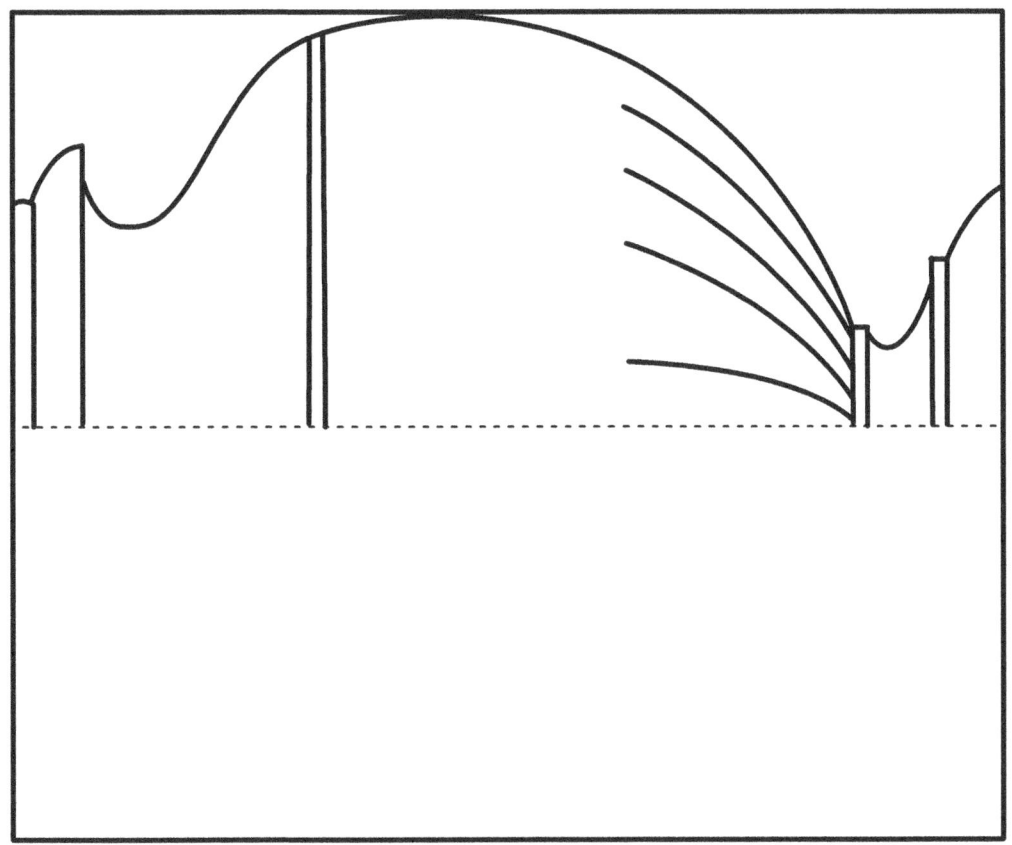

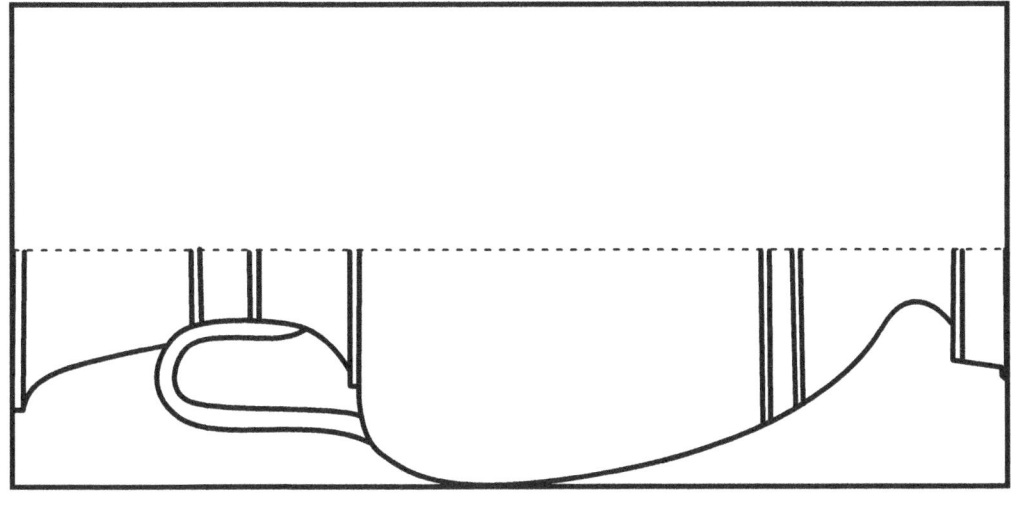

SYMMETRICAL DRAWING

Here are some fun designs to try to imitate. Use the boxes to guide you through the process of drawing these symmetrical designs. Have fun!

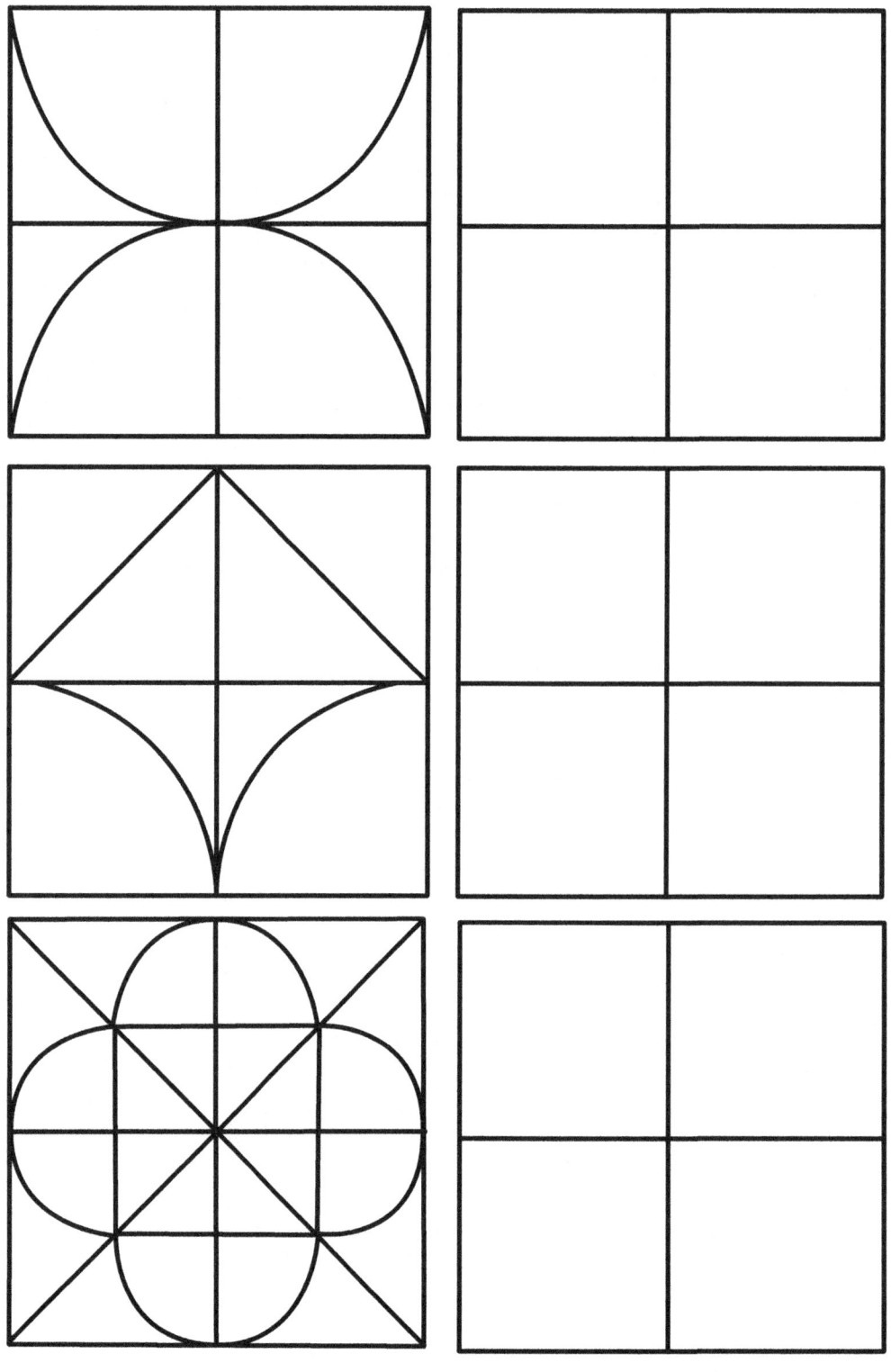

SYMMETRICAL DRAWING

Here are some fun designs to try to imitate. Use the boxes to guide you through the process of drawing these symmetrical designs. Have fun!

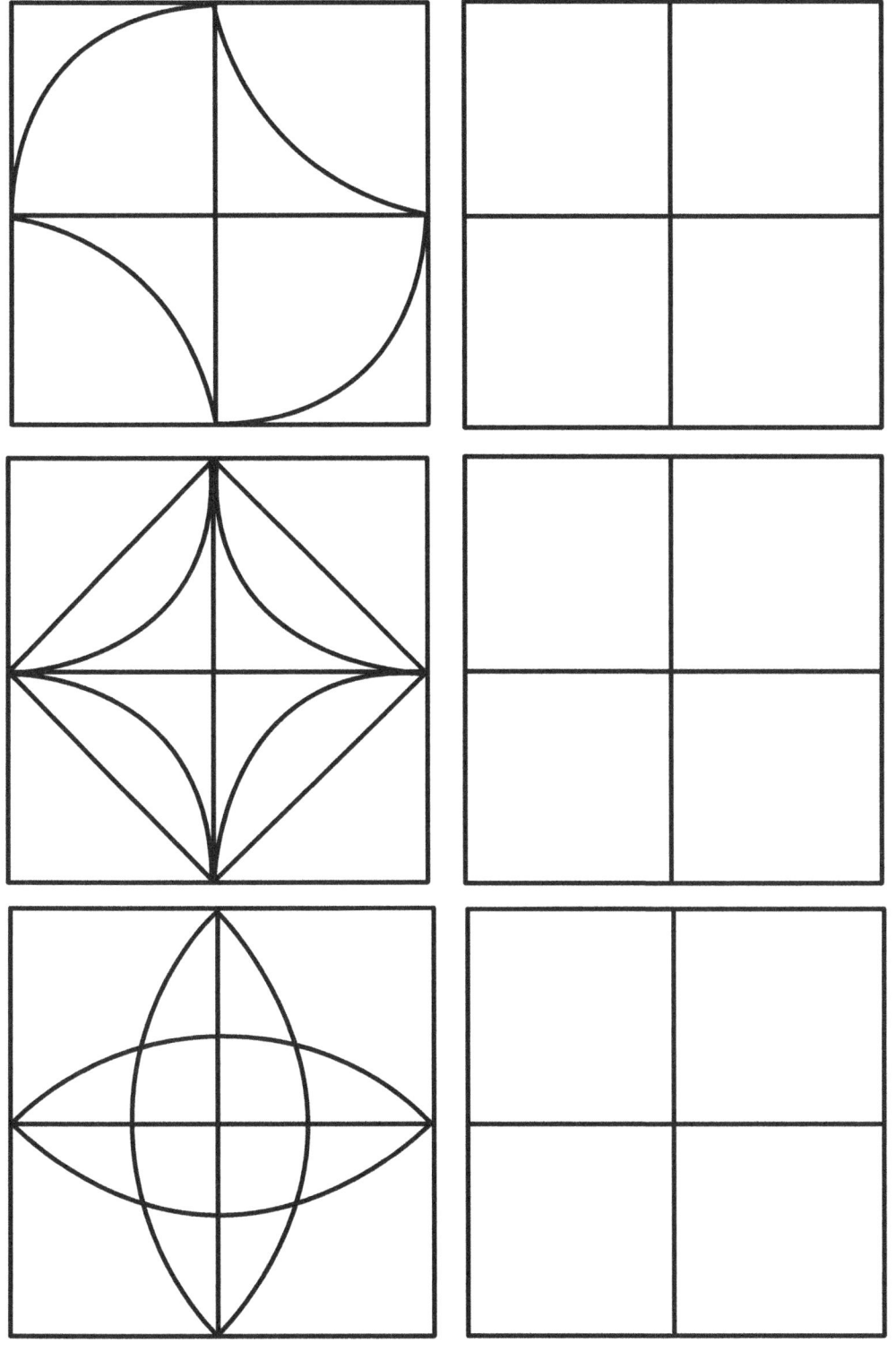

SYMMETRICAL DRAWING

Here are some fun designs to try to imitate. Use the boxes to guide you through the process of drawing these symmetrical designs. Have fun!

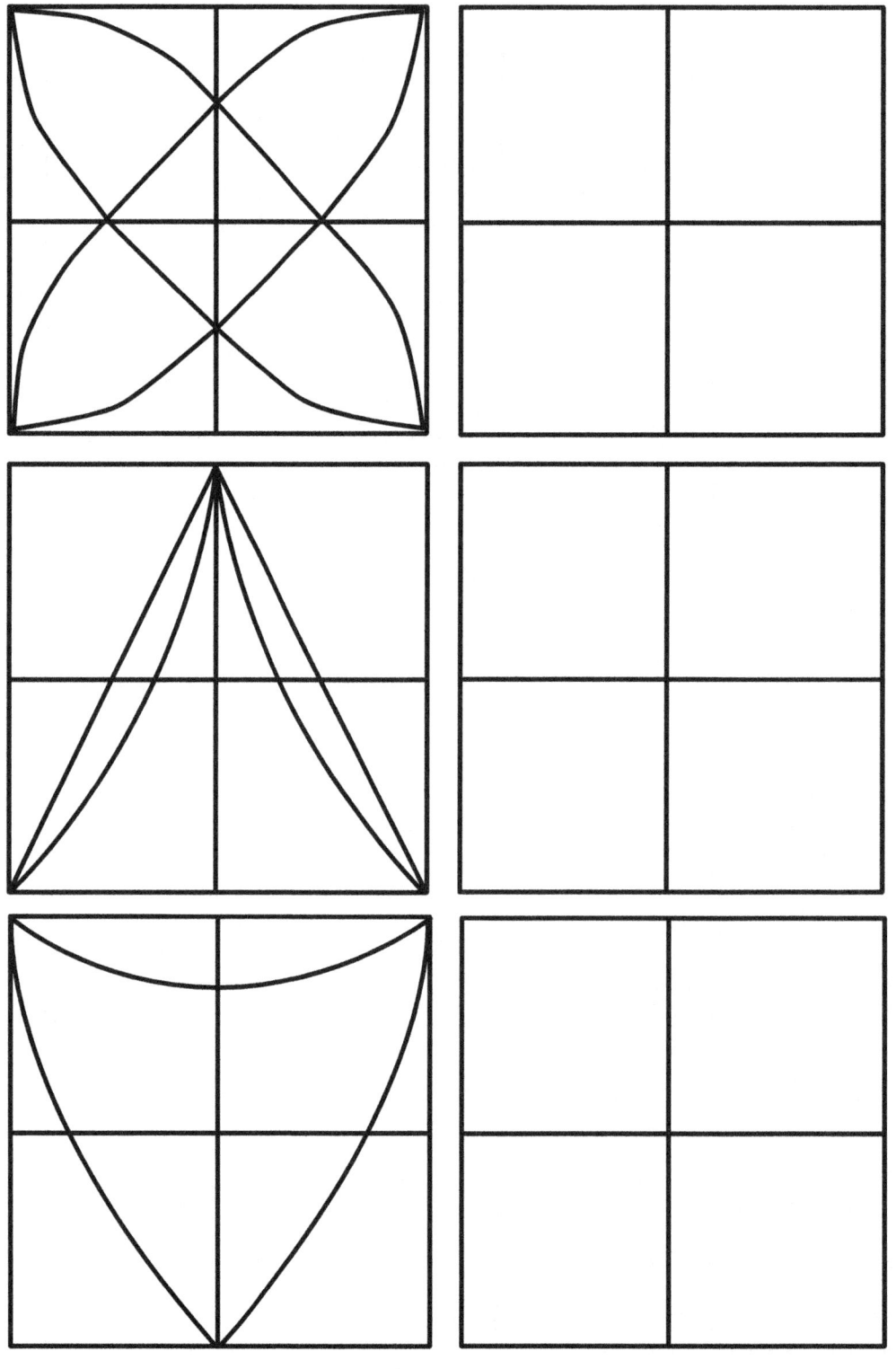

SYMMETRICAL DRAWING

Here are some fun designs to try to imitate. Use the boxes to guide you through the process of drawing these symmetrical designs. Have fun!

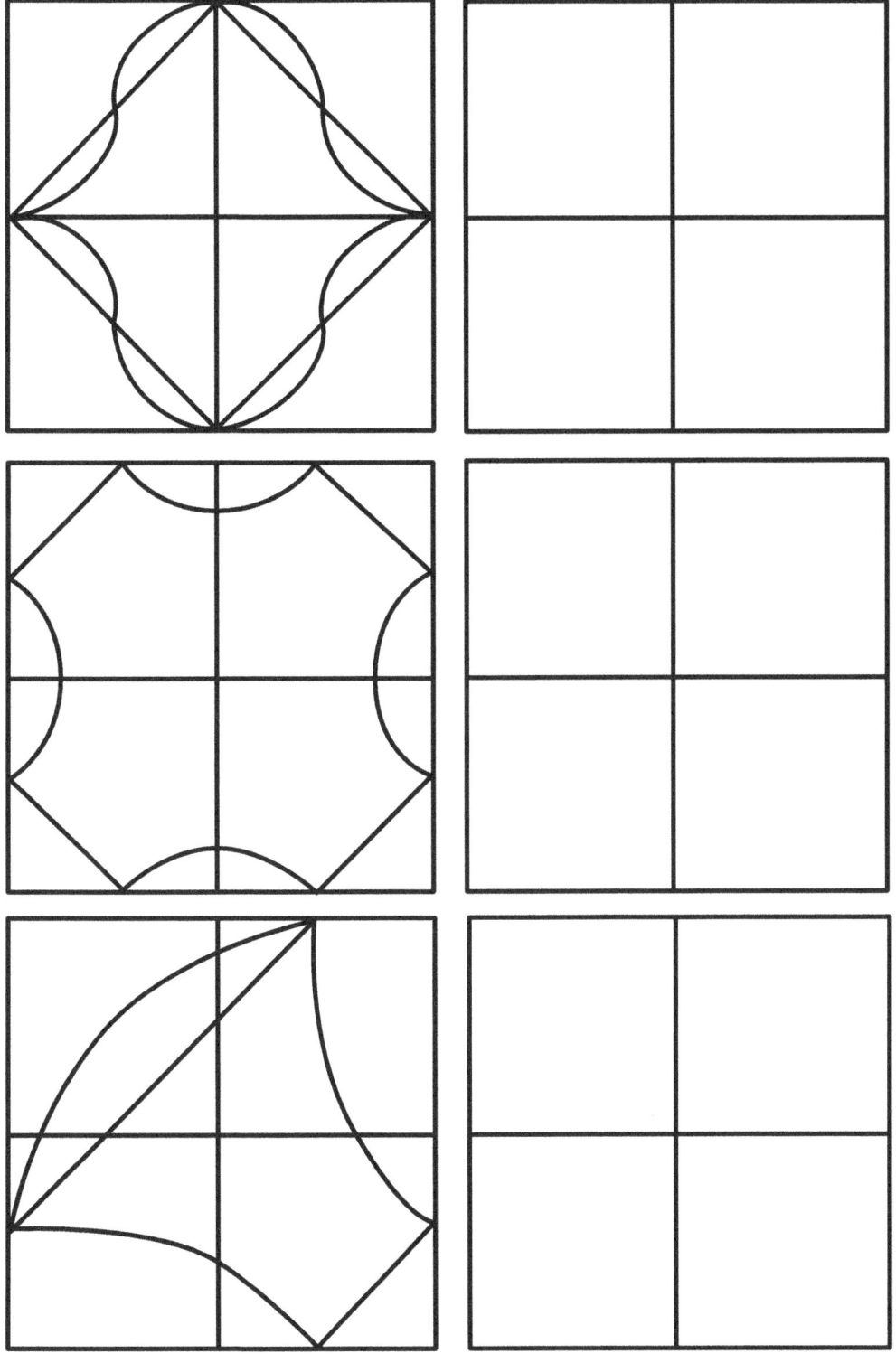

ZENTANGLES FUN

What are Zentangles? Well Zentangles are an easy way to relax and just have fun with drawing structured patterns. It sounds boring but it is a fun way to provide yourself with some creative fun!

You start with some geometric shapes

Then you fill the empty spaces with various patterns

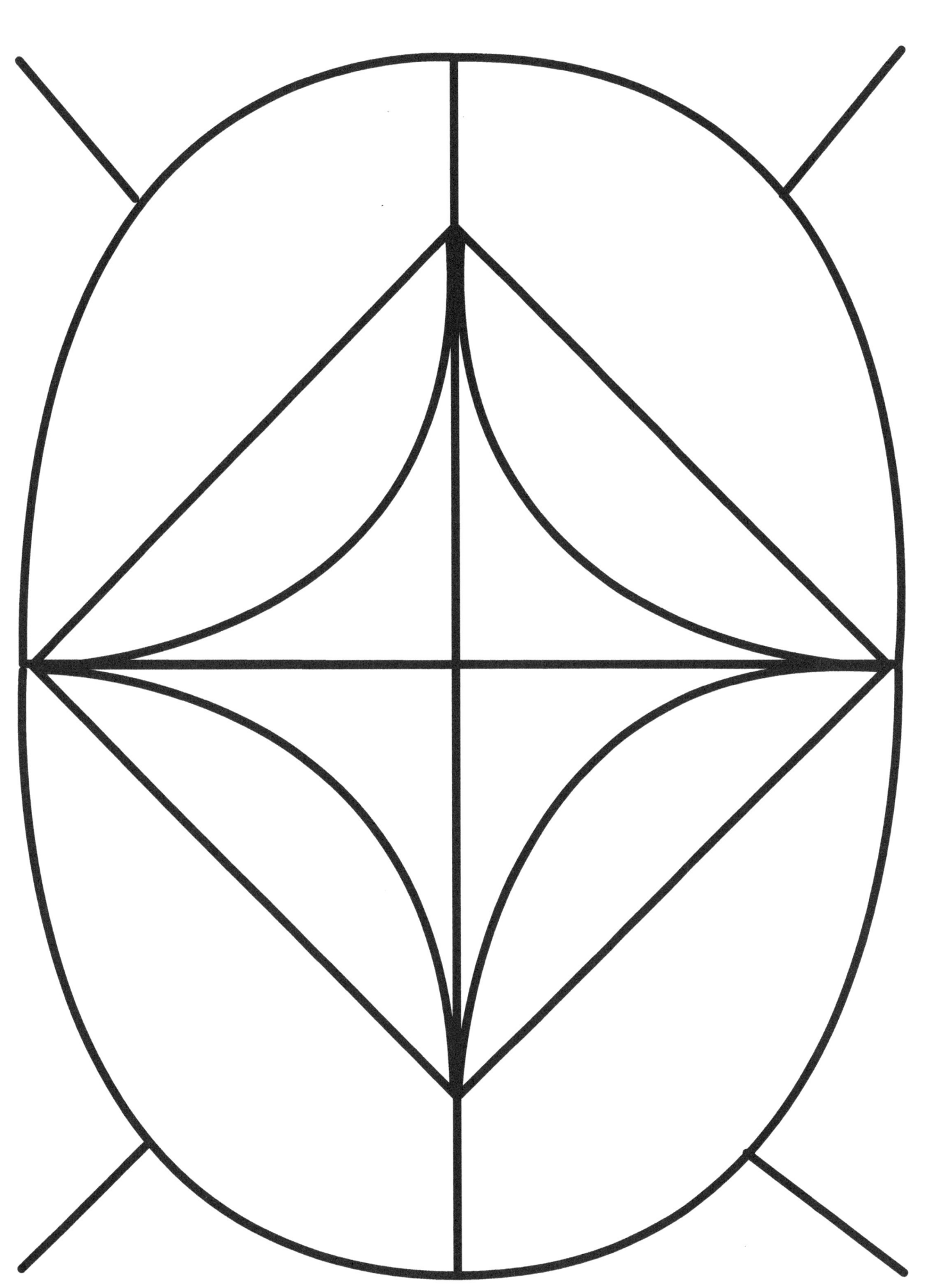

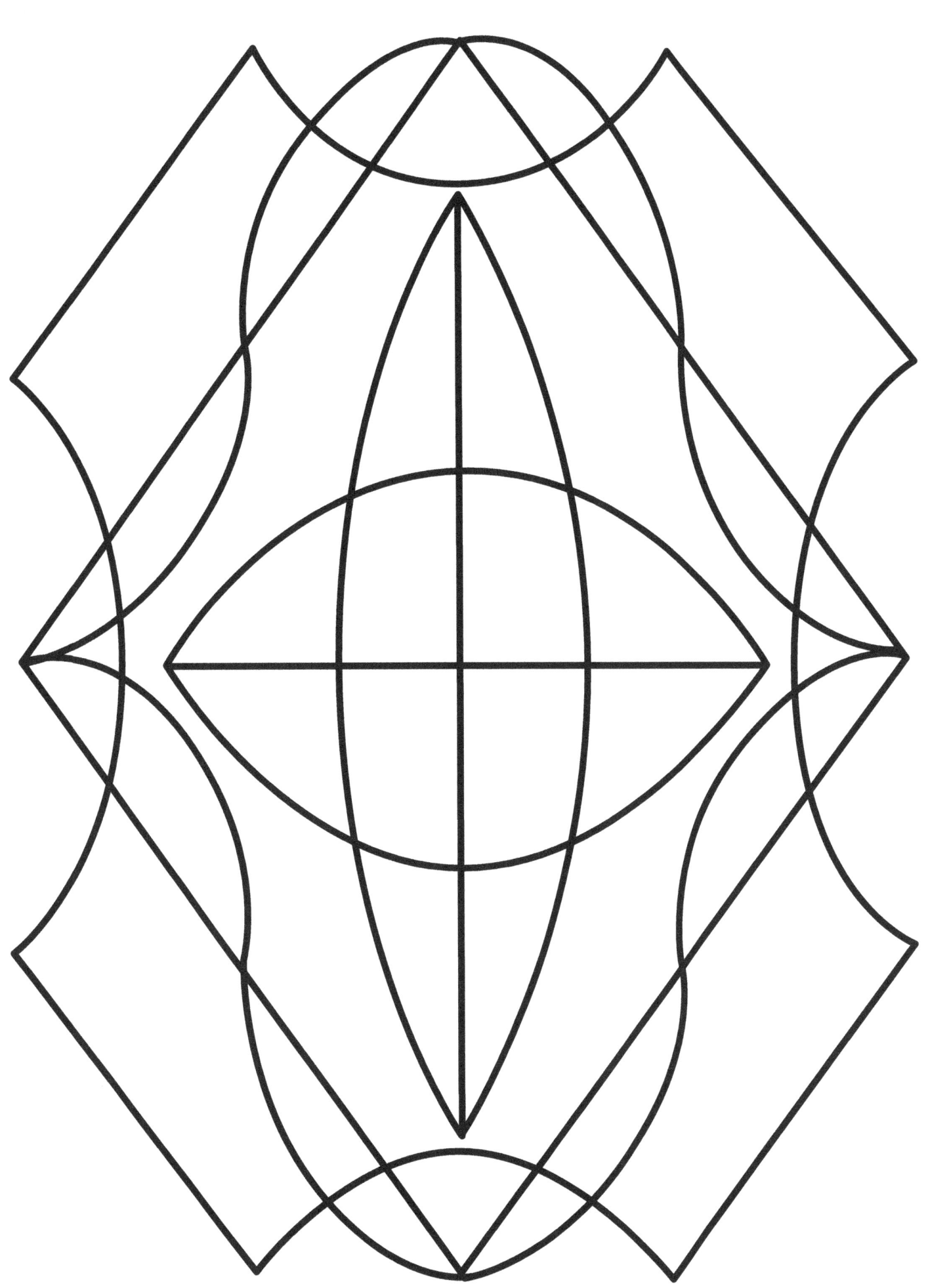

FUN WITH EYES

Finish these pictures... draw people, animals, or creatures with these silly eyes to spark your creativity.

FUN WITH EYES

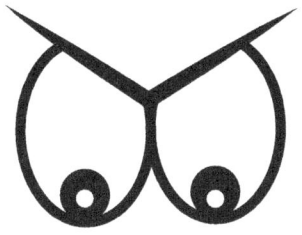

FUN WITH MOUTHS

Finish these pictures... draw people or creatures with these silly mouths to spark your creativity.

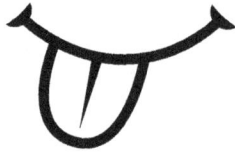

FUN WITH MOUTHS

Finish these pictures... draw people or creatures with these silly mouths to spark your creativity.

FUN WITH FACES

Finish these faces by using your creativity!

FUN WITH FACES

Finish these faces by using your creativity!

FUN WITH FACES

Finish these faces by using your creativity!

FUN WITH FACES

Finish these faces by using your creativity!

FUN WITH FACES

Finish these faces by using your creativity!

SHARED DOODLE GAME

This game is so much fun. My daughter and I play it and we always draw very silly things in order to make each other laugh. This is how you play:

This can be played with 2 or more players. Set a timer for 5 or 10 minutes. Then pass the paper back and forth between you and the other player(s). Each person draws one thing before passing the paper to the player on the right. Keep passing to the right, each player drawing another thing, until the timer dings.

Set the timer to 5 or 10 minutes.

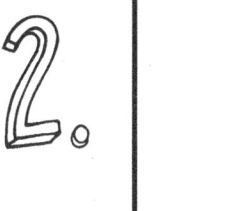 

The first person should draw one item on the paper.

SHARED DOODLE GAME

  Pass the paper to the right and let the next player add something to the paper.

  Continue to pass the paper to the right and let the next player add something to the paper.

  When the buzzer rings, then your drawing is complete. Share it with each other and laugh at its silliness.

THREE CARDS GAME

Here is a fun game to play with friends or alone. This game often ends in a hilarious picture. The game is very simple.

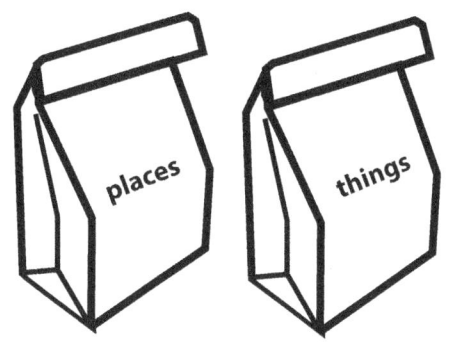

1. Cut out the cards on the following pages.

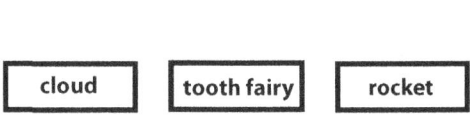

2. Put the "places" cards in one of the bags and place the "things" cards in the other bag.

3. Pick one "places" card and two "things" cards (without peeking).

4. Draw the picture including all 3 of these items. Let the laughing start.

GARDEN	SCHOOL
PLAYGROUND	KITCHEN
JUNGLE	PARIS
BEDROOM	PRISON
BEACH	OCEAN
HOSPITAL	NEW YORK CITY
GROCERY STORE	TREE HOUSE
MEDIEVAL TIMES	SPACE SHIP
ON THE MOON	OUTER SPACE
IN THE FUTURE	EGYPT

WILD WEST	UNDER THE SEA
DOCTOR'S OFFICE	RESTAURANT
SCIENCE LAB	PET STORE
THE WHITE HOUSE	AMUSEMENT PARK
PARADE	FAIR OR CARNIVAL
CITY	ON A SHIP OR BOAT
INSIDE A CAR	FARM
SUMMER SCENE	ON A CLOUD
BIRTHDAY PARTY	WINTER SCENE
CAFETERIA	HALLOWEEN TIME

HAMBURGER	BALLOON
TRUCK	CAR
BABY	BOAT
PIG	CROCODILE
DOG	CAT
APPLE	CANOE
HOUSE	MOM
DAD	ZOMBIE
SISTER	BROTHER
TEACHER	BOOK

COMPUTER	BALL
GLOVE	VACUUM
COUCH	DESK
PIG	CROCODILE
EASEL	LADDER
HEART	SHOVEL
SHOE	BUCKET
CLOWN	COWBOY
ASTRONAUT	PRINCESS
PRINCE	QUEEN

LAWYER	DOCTOR
BOSS	PIRATE
VIKING	SOLDIER
PRESIDENT	STUDENT
MAILMAN	POLICE MAN/WOMAN
FIREMAN	LIBRARIAN
SCIENTIST	REPORTER
MONSTER	OGRE
TEDDY BEAR	ZEBRA
GIRAFFE	FROG

SNAKE	BIRD
REINDEER	COW
BUNNY	RAT
HAMSTER	MONKEY
APE	DUCK
FOX	WOLF
OSTRICH	COMET
METEOR	ROCKET
FIRE	WATER
PLANET	VOLCANO

ORANGE	FIREPLACE
FAN	CHOCOLATE
UNICORN	HORSE
GIFT	MAILBOX
GREETING CARD	TOOTH FAIRY
DINOSAUR	DRAGON
SAW	CURLY HAIR
OCTOPUS	FLOWER
SANTA CLAUS	ELF
FAIRY	EASTER BUNNY

WRITE IN YOUR OWN THINGS	

WRITE IN YOUR OWN THINGS	

WRITE IN YOUR OWN THINGS	

BACK AND FORTH GAME

This game is great for parties of children, or as little as 2 children. Each player sits, pencil in hand, before a blank sheet of paper, his object being to make a picture containing things chosen by the first player before him. The first player then names the thing that he wants in the picture. Perhaps it is a tree. He therefore says, "Draw a tree," then all the players, himself included, draws a tree. Perhaps the next says, "Draw a monkey climbing the tree"; the next, "Draw a kite caught in the top branches"; the next, "Draw two little babies looking up at the kite"; and so on, until the picture is full enough. It is fun seeing how everybody's pictures are so different, even though everybody had the same instructions. Have fun!!!

PICK YOUR FACE

This game can be played alone or with your friends. Either way, the pictures that are drawn from this game are so much fun to see!!!

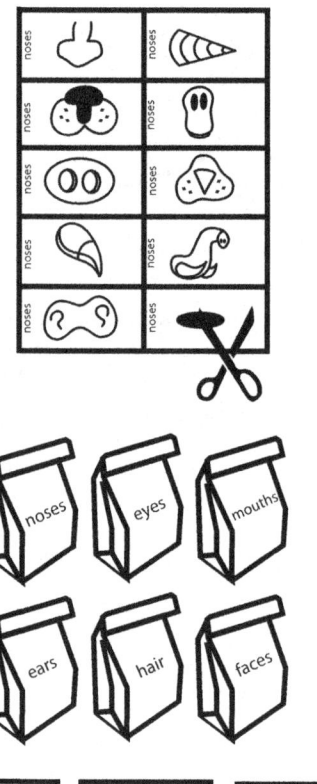

1. Cut out the cards on the following pages.

2. Put each category of cards into a separate bag.

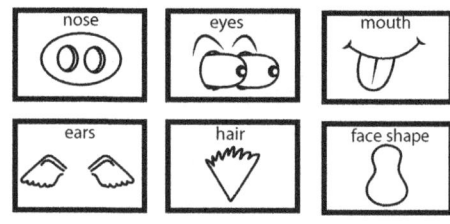

3. Pick one card from each bag.

4. Draw the crazy face that your card choices have told you to draw.

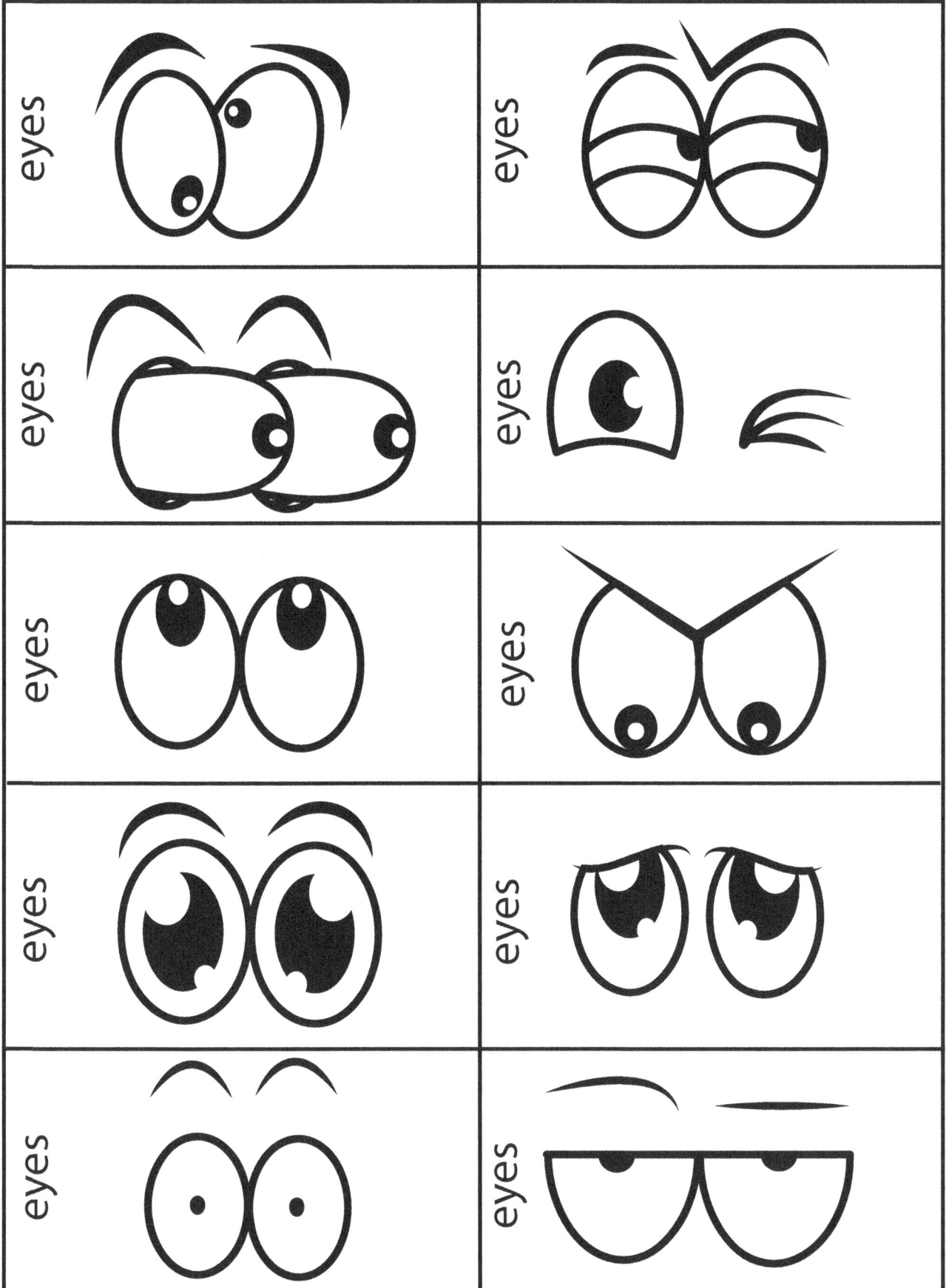

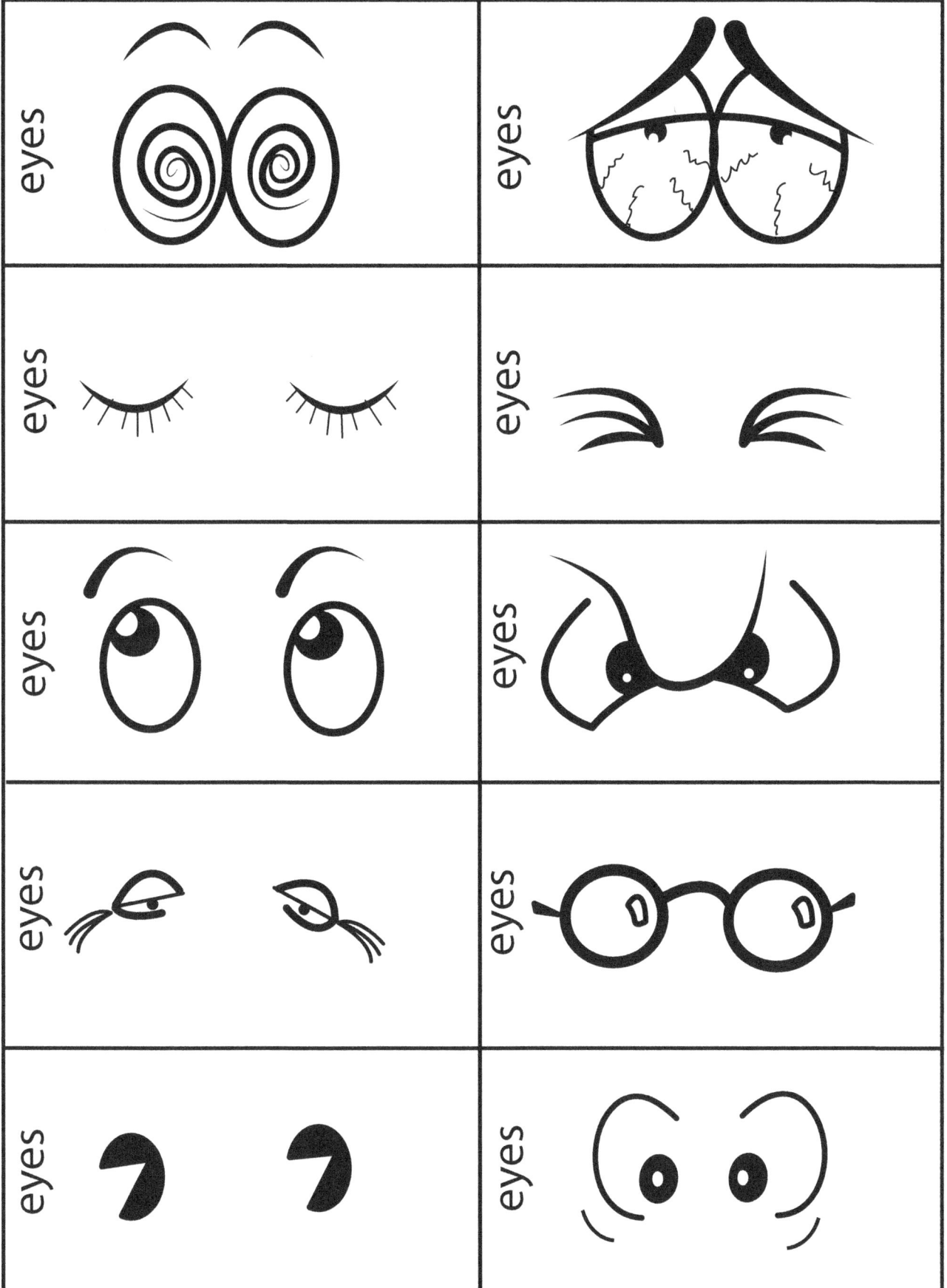

noses	noses	noses	noses	noses
noses	noses	noses	noses	noses

noses	noses
noses	noses
noses	noses
noses	noses
noses	noses

mouths	mouths	mouths	mouths	mouths
mouths	mouths	mouths	mouths	mouths

mouths	mouths
mouths	mouths
mouths	mouths
mouths	mouths
mouths	mouths

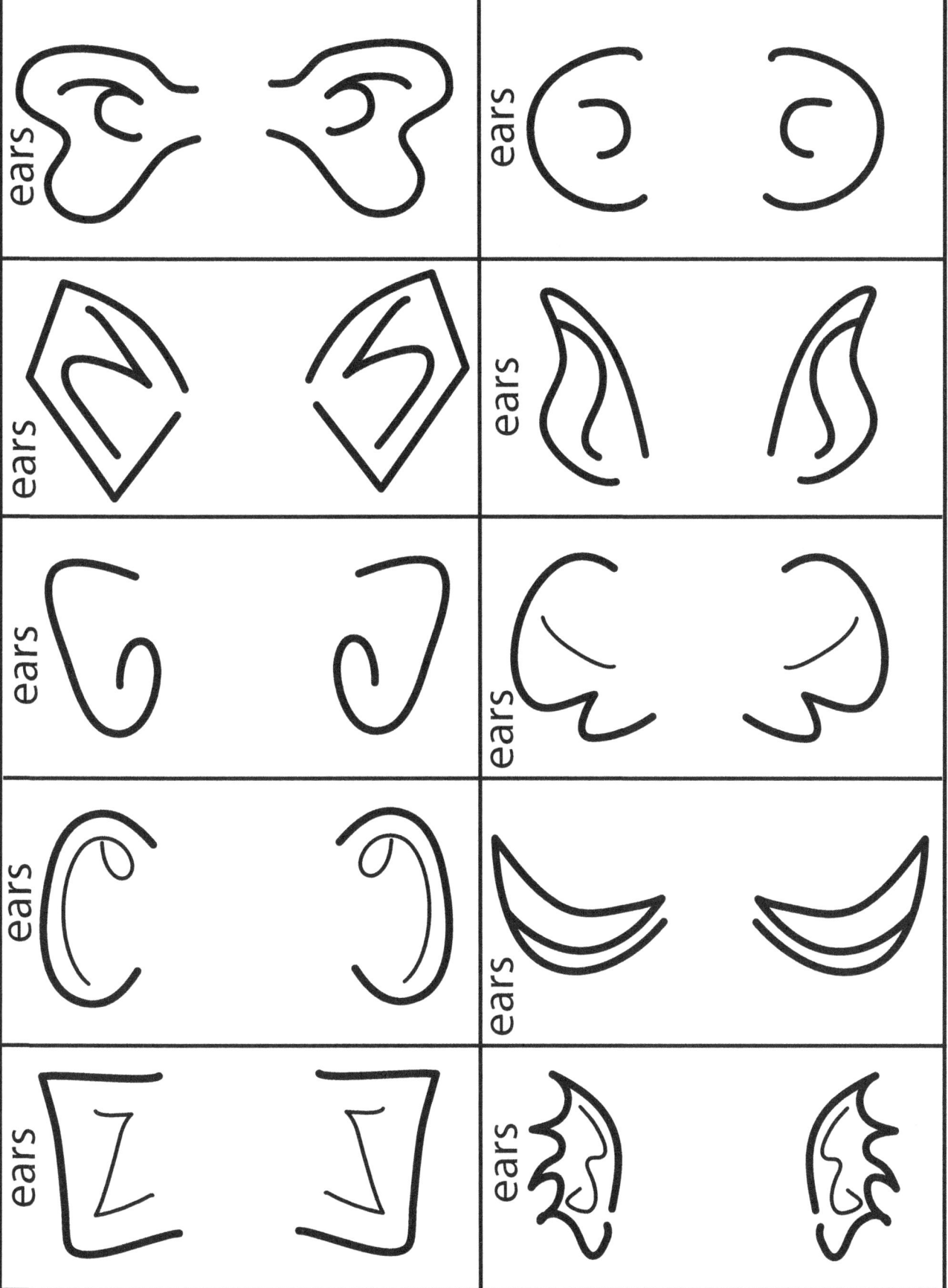

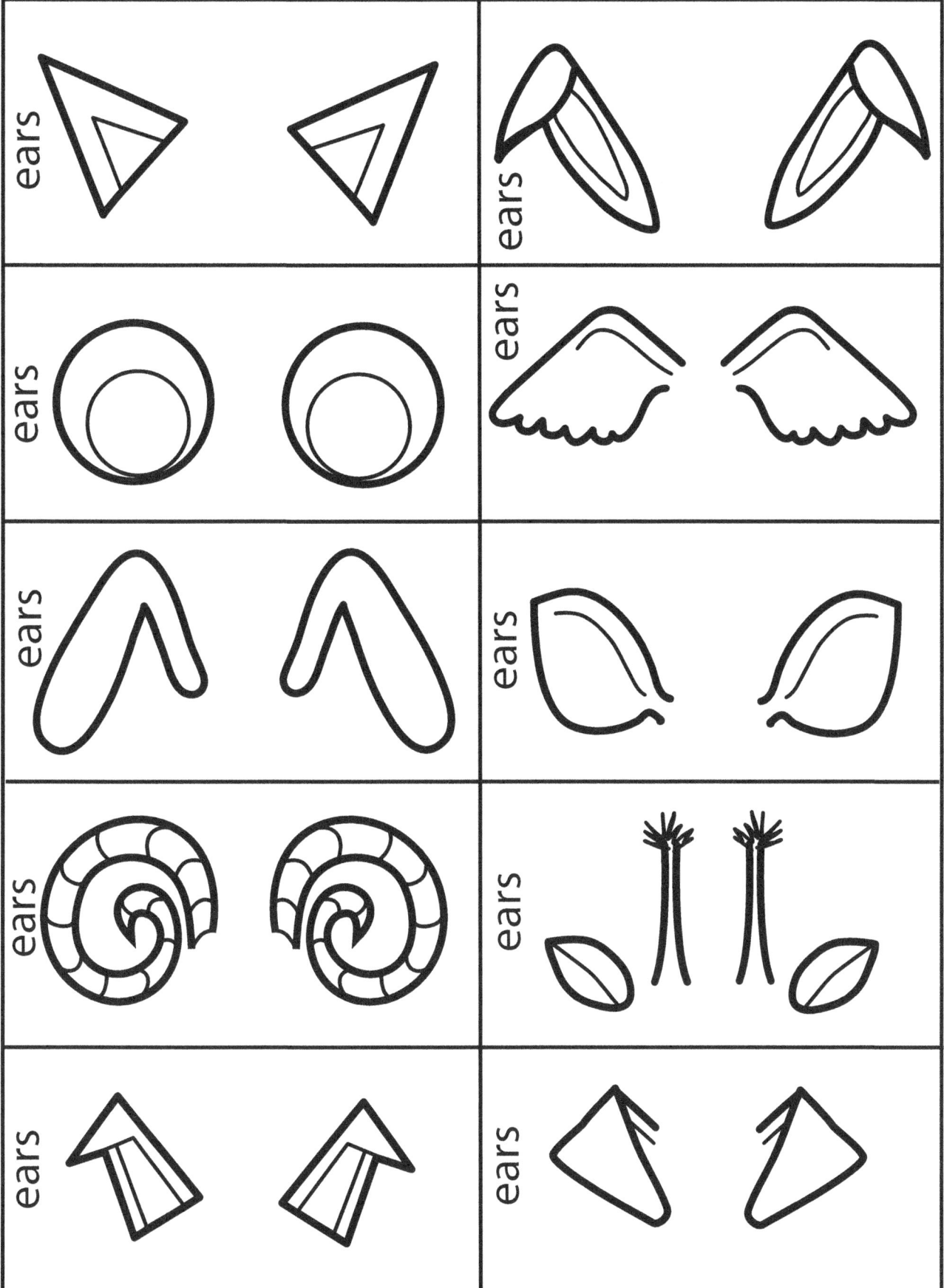

hair / hats	hair / hats
hair / hats	hair / hats
hair / hats	hair / hats
hair / hats	hair / hats
hair / hats	hair / hats

hair / hats	hair / hats
hair / hats	hair / hats
hair / hats	hair / hats
hair / hats	hair / hats
hair / hats	hair / hats

faces	faces
faces	faces
faces	faces
faces	faces
faces	faces

DRAWING SIMON SAYS

This is a version of "Simon Says" that is fun for all. Instead of doing physical activities, in this version, you draw instead. Here is how you play this version.

The leader calls out the orders that the follower must follow in order to win. *(The leader secretly draws his picture ahead of time.)* Here are some examples:
- Simon says draw a large circle.
- Simon says draw a triangle nose inside that circle.
- Draw a square body.
- Simon says draw circles for eyes.

The follower should only follow orders that start with "Simon Says"...otherwise the follower should ignore that order. So, in the example above, the follower would draw a circle with a triangle nose and circle eyes. However, the follower should NOT draw a square body (because the leader did NOT say "Simon Says".)

At the end of the game, the Leader compares his picture with the follower's picture to see if the follower followed the instructions correctly.

3D SHAPES

Do you want to know how to make 3-dimensional shapes? Here is a really easy way to create the 3d effect that you're looking for.

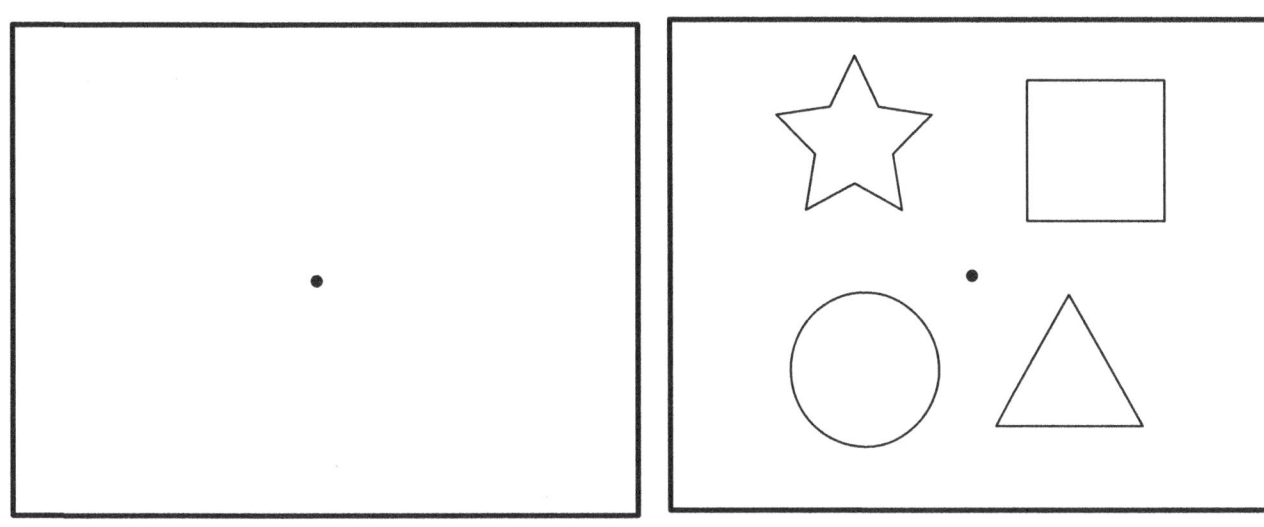

Draw a dot in the center of the page. Then draw some shapes around the dot.

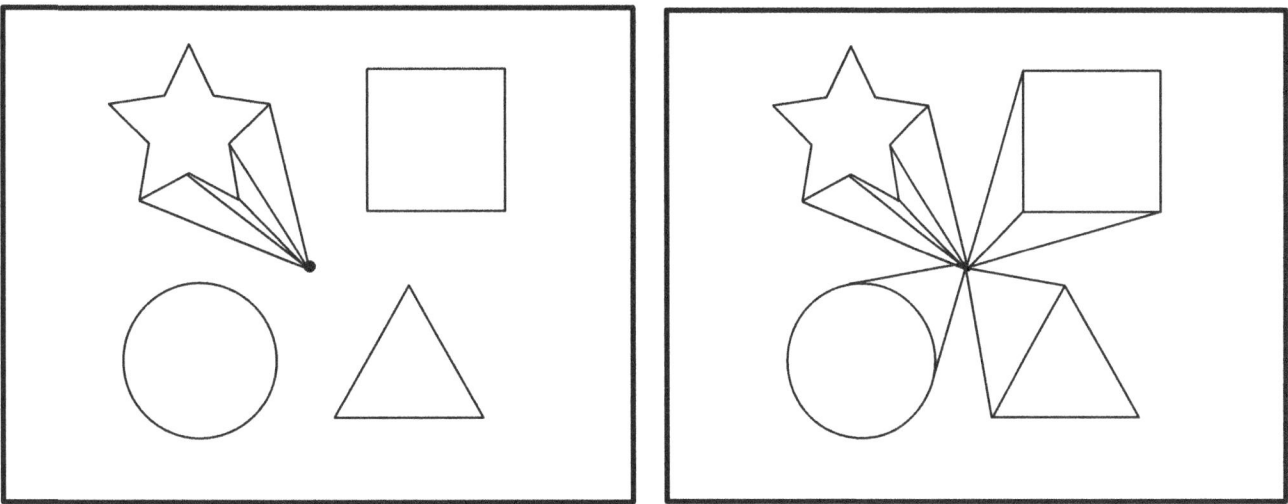

Then just draw lines from all the inner edges of the shapes towards the dot, as I have above. It will create a 3d effect!

BUBBLE LETTERS

Lightly draw your letters ... draw them any way you like. If you want them to be perfect, you can use a ruler to draw boxes first and then draw your letters inside of them.

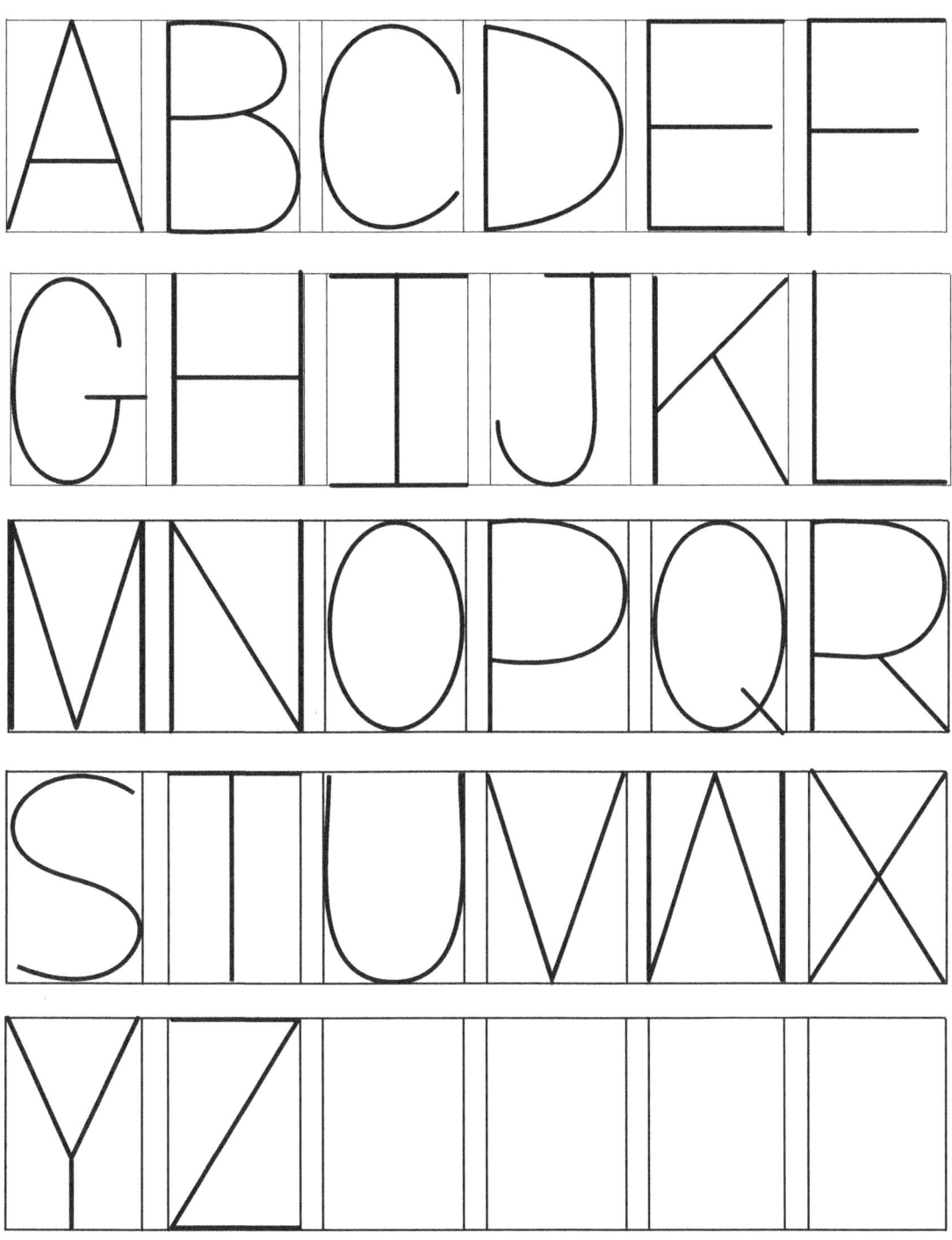

BUBBLE LETTERS

Now just outline the letters with rounded edges. Have fun with it and don't get stressed out trying to make it exactly like I did.

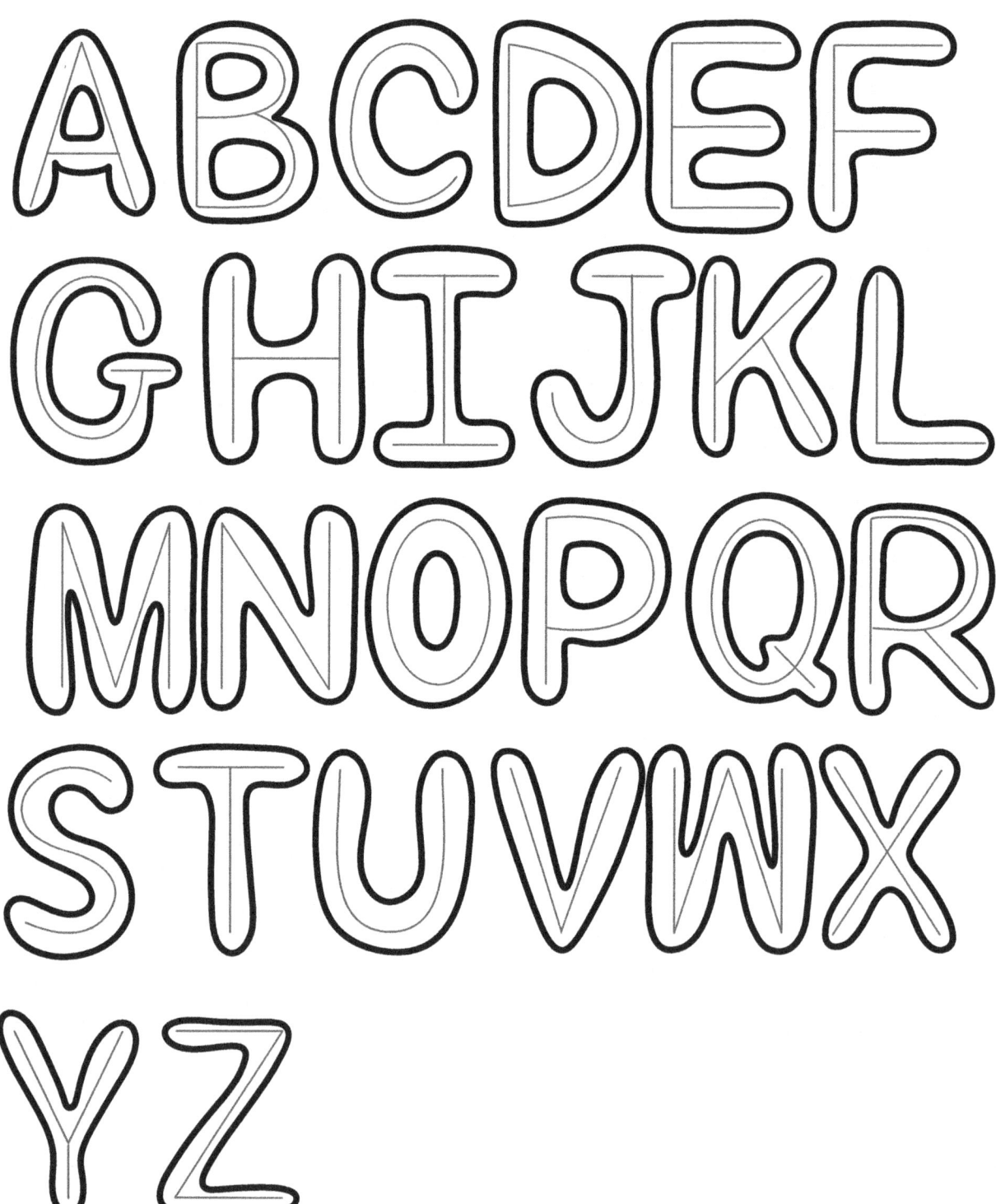

BUBBLE LETTERS

Don't feel like drawing your own letters first? No problem, use these letters to practice on. Outline these letters with curved lines...just like we did on the previous page.

A B C D E F
G H I J K L
M N O P Q R
S T U V W X
Y Z

BUBBLE LETTERS

Now add shadow lines to the right side of the letters...as we did below.

ABCDEF
GHIJKL
MNOPQR
STUVWX
YZ

BUBBLE LETTERS

Now just add ovals to the left side of each bubble letter...for the highlights.

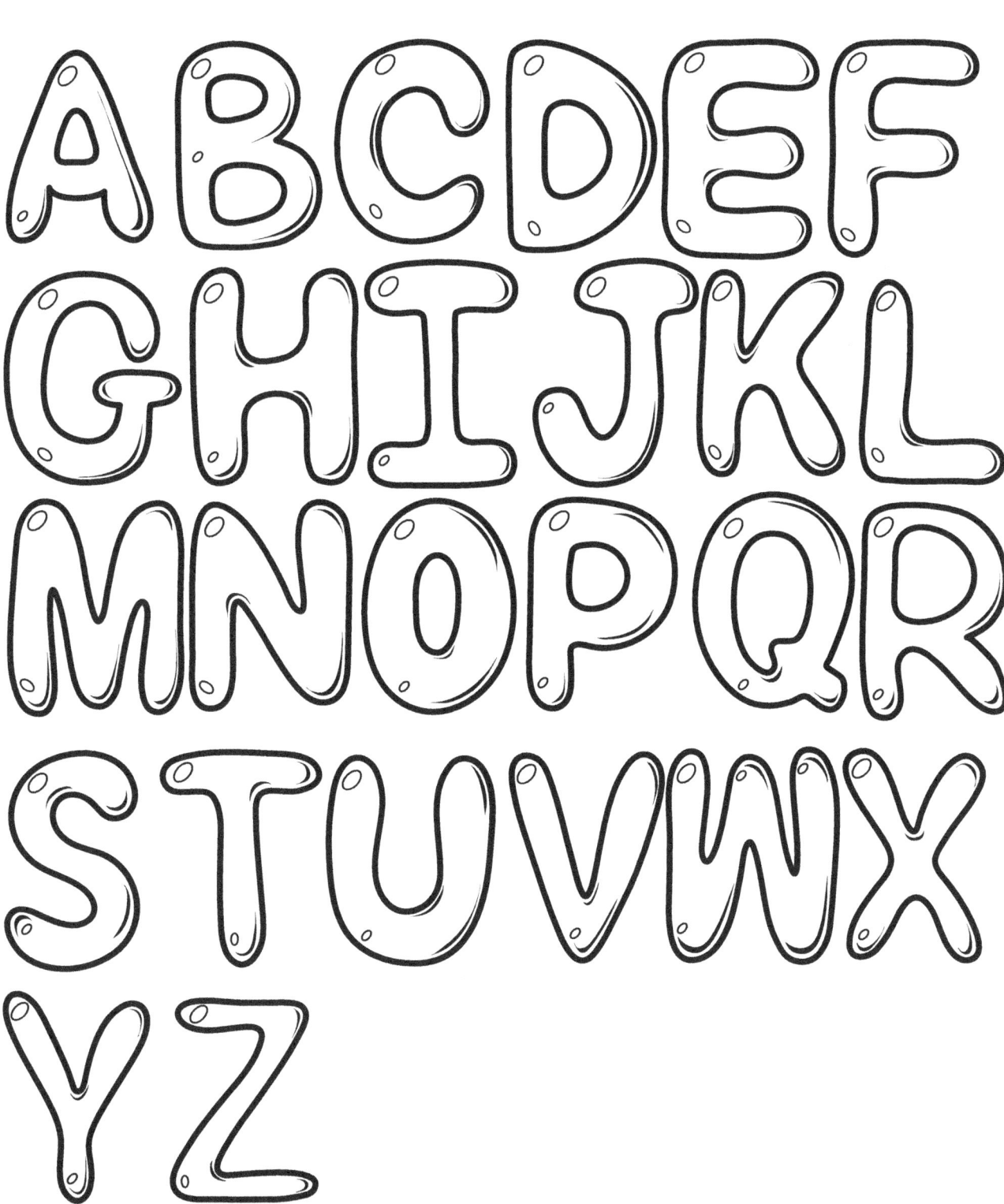

BUBBLE LETTERS

Didn't feel like drawing the bubble letters either? No problem...we did it for you. Draw the shadow lines and the highlight ovals. Have fun!

OUR OTHER BOOKS

Please Give Us Good Reviews on Amazon! If you like it, we will put together another games book. **If You Give us a 5 Star Review**, and Email us About it, We Will Do a Tutorial Per Your Child's Request and Post it On DrawingHowToDraw.com

Made in the USA
Monee, IL
17 January 2021